How to Escape the No-Win Trap

BARBARA COWAN BERG

Barbara Cowan Berg

McGraw-Hill

New York   Chicago   San Francisco   Lisbon   London
Madrid   Mexico City   Milan   New Delhi   San Juan
Seoul   Singapore   Sydney   Toronto

Copyright © 2004 by Barbara Cowan Berg. All rights reserved. Printed in the United States of America. Except as permitted under the United States Copyright Act of 1976, no part of this publication may be reproduced or distributed in any form or by any means, or stored in a database or retrieval system, without the prior written permission of the publisher.

1 2 3 4 5 6 7 8 9 0   DOC/DOC   0 1 0 9 8 7 6 5 4

ISBN 0-07-142361-3

The purpose of this book is to educate. It is sold with the understanding that the author and publisher shall have neither liability nor responsibility for any injury caused or alleged to be caused directly or indirectly by the information in this book. While every effort has been made to ensure the book's accuracy, its contents should not be construed as medical advice. Each person's health needs are unique. To obtain recommendations appropriate to your particular situation, please consult a qualified health-care professional.

All names, descriptions, and situations, have been altered to protect the confidentiality and privacy of clients and others with whom the author has worked.

McGraw-Hill books are available at special quantity discounts to use as premiums and sales promotions, or for use in corporate training programs. For more information, please write to the Director of Special Sales, Professional Publishing, McGraw-Hill, Two Penn Plaza, New York, NY 10121-2298. Or contact your local bookstore.

 This book is printed on recycled, acid-free paper containing a minimum of 50% recycled, de-inked fiber.

Library of Congress Cataloging-in-Publication Data

Berg, Barbara Cowan.
   How to escape the no-win trap / Barbara A. Berg.
     p. cm.
   Includes bibliographical references and index.
   ISBN 0-07-142361-3 (alk. paper)
    1. Decision making. 2. Double bind (Psychology) I. Title.
  BF448.B46 2004
  158—dc22
                                2003018142

To my daughter, Brittany

And for everyone and anyone who has ever
gotten tired of taking the brunt of everything
and hopes there can be another way

Contents

Acknowledgments

*M*y parents will always be in my heart for showing me the importance of being true to myself and never losing sight of my dreams. My clients in private practice and my workshop participants are also a great inspiration, as they have shared their dreams and hurts along with the hurdles they have worked on overcoming, so as to side step the no-win traps in their lives.

I would like to express my sincere gratitude to my editor at McGraw-Hill, Nancy Hancock, who saw the potential of this project and directed me to produce a book on the subject of no-win traps that went beyond the level of depth and insight I had originally imagined. Much thanks also to everyone I had the privilege of working with at McGraw-Hill. This includes, but is not limited to, Meg Leder, Jane Palmieri, and Ann Pryor.

It has been my good fortune to have Ken Atchity of AEI as my literary manager. His guidance and steadfast commitment to this project made sure it would be well placed. Also, much appreciation and gratitude goes to David Angsten with The Writer's Lifeline, Inc., for his brilliant editing and input. Without Michele Witte's diligent administrative help, this project would not have happened; and Kathi Van Hassel Abbey provided excellent input as well. Much thanks goes to Nancy Cortez, Lili Sandor-Troy, and Daun White for their caring assistance and attention to details.

I also want to thank Don and Bette Brown for their continual support and direction in my self-expression and delivery of the messages I have to convey, along with the ever-inspiring Paul Ryan, who never lets me quit or let myself down.

With great regard for my mentors and guides in my own transformation and development, I want to thank Kathy Johnson; Morgan

Hartt; Al Shane; Rabyn Judith Pillsbury; Santokh Singh Khalsa, D.C.; Sat Nam Kaur Khalsa; and Dawn Lane Baker.

Regarding the personal side of my life, I am forever grateful and delighted to have as my two best friends, travel buddies, and daily conversants Liz Roman and Dr. Marsha Krohn. Thanks to the following colleagues and friends, I have weathered my own life's dilemmas and found safe harbors when the going got particularly rough: Janelle Killingsworth, Harriett Guttman, Judi Faye, Sharon O'Neill, Don Davenport, Alma L. Visser, and Connie Conard.

And ever so much thanks and appreciation for George, who has brought me the gift of finally having both love in my heart and work that I love, all at the same time. I'm no longer stuck in the trap of thinking I can only have one or the other.

Barbara Cowan Berg

Introduction

It seemed like a good idea at the time. . . .

Many of us spend much of our lives trying to please someone who is impossible to please or trying to solve a predicament that no one could solve, only to end up feeling like failures, unworthy of love or success. Looking at life from this point of view is a "no-win trap"—it leaves us with no way to win.

The frustrating dilemma of a no-win trap, also known as a "double bind," is that it requires us to make an impossible choice between equally undesirable alternatives. We feel trapped, unable to escape, and at the same time, compelled to do *something*. It's easy to see how continuous battle with these impossible situations drains our energy, demolishes our self-esteem, and keeps us enmeshed and unable to grow.

This book offers an answer to the no-win trap. It presents a method where endlessly trying over and over the same way is finally recognized as not only unnecessary, but part of the problem itself.

In these times of constant change, sensory overload, and troubling uncertainty, we are compelled to make the wisest possible choices at every turn, even if there appears to be no actual "choice" at the time. But life doesn't have to be so difficult or complicated. There is a way to approach yourself, others, and almost any situation so that smarter decisions are more easily made, allowing you to pull yourself out of trouble before you've gotten in too far, or turn things around when there seems no way to win.

It's time to be successful in the everyday business of life. Success isn't about never making mistakes—it's about proactively changing course when you see yourself moving in a direction that has no chance of lasting satisfaction. The next eight chapters will take you on a journey that will help you assess where you are now in your life, how you got there, and what you can do to step out or detach yourself from predicaments that don't work for you. Read on for a better way to live, with less grief and havoc, and new insights for yourself and those around you.

1

Understanding the World of No-Win Traps

People only see what they are prepared to see.

Ralph Waldo Emerson

*E*ven when you know where you want to go and believe the odds are in your favor, life can present you with daunting challenges. One of the most persistent and difficult challenges is the no-win trap, the "double bind" dilemma that seems to thwart you in every direction and sends you bouncing back and forth like a Ping-Pong ball. These baffling dilemmas offer no obvious or acceptable solution, and often lead you to feel angry and misunderstood, or so totally overwhelmed and out of control that you see no end or safe haven in sight and just want to give up altogether.

But you can't. Or at least you *believe* you can't.

And that is the key to the situation. I know this from my own life, and from clients and others. I've learned, quite often the hard way, that I stay in dilemmas longer when I'm totally focused on the problem, instead of on my attitude or approach to the problem. Whatever that problem is, however uncomfortable or horrendous it may be, it *can* be solved if you're willing to make changes. You don't have to give up; you just need to give up acting the way you've been acting and thinking the way you've been thinking.

This is obviously easier said than done, especially when it feels like there's no way out. But consider the following point:

Currently, you're probably in at least one major life situation where you feel wrong no matter what you do. The odds are, you've found yourself in difficult, intractable positions like this one before, and you have wondered why this always seems to keep happening to you.

If this rings true to your experience, take a moment to consider this:

Chances are, the no-win dilemma you're experiencing is in large part determined by the way you see yourself—the person you have come to believe yourself to be—in your dealings with people and with life in general. It often seems that if you could just get rid of "problem people" or "rotten situations," your life would be just fine; but in fact your no-win dilemma may have less to do with difficult people and situations, and more to do with how you respond to them.

It is truly amazing that so many of us can spend so much of our lives wondering, "What's a nice person like me doing in a situation like this?" and "How did I ever get here?" I certainly know I have.

While it may appear as if everyone else is the issue and you're only an innocent bystander, this book will effectively and lovingly help you step back and "watch the movie of your life"—to view yourself from the outside in this "scene" and others like it. You will come to be able to observe your situation as *a process to learn from* rather than as one more reason to beat up on yourself and others. As you begin to develop this capacity, you'll be moving away from frustration and chaos and toward peacefulness and enjoyment of the person you really are.

Over time, you'll gain poise and a sense of timing concerning when to put your energy, heart, and soul into another person or situation, and when to step back and detach. As you gain understanding of insights, concepts, and options for dealing with the curveballs life seems to bring your way, you'll more easily recognize how and why a particular dilemma seems to bring you overwhelming stress when you had hoped it would bring you only joy. You'll have some genuine epiphanies as you realize that you no longer need to be imprisoned in impossible situations as if your life depended on it. You'll then be able to successfully recognize where to put your efforts and where you'll most likely only get drained. Even more satisfaction will be yours when you are able to recognize scenarios you might have fallen for before, but now it would never occur to you to fall into them one more time.

And that's the crux of the no-win trap: knowing when to "keep trying" as you have been, and when it's time to alter course or let go altogether. It's often difficult to tell where actual choices led to the situation and where the curveballs of life come into play. To gain insight into how you may have knowingly or unknowingly fallen into a trap, consider the following simple yet insightful poem by Portia Nelson, from *There's a Hole in My Sidewalk* (Beyond Words Publishing, Inc., Hillsboro, Oregon, 1993):

Autobiography in Five Short Chapters

CHAPTER ONE

I walk down the street.
> There is a deep hole in the sidewalk.
> I fall in.
> I am lost . . . I am helpless.
>> It isn't my fault.
It takes forever to find a way out.

CHAPTER TWO

I walk down the same street.
> There is a deep hole in the sidewalk.
> I pretend I don't see it.
> I fall in again.
I can't believe I am in the same place.
>> But, it isn't my fault.
It still takes a long time to get out.

CHAPTER THREE

I walk down the same street.
There is a deep hole in the sidewalk.
I *see* it is there.
I still fall in. . . . It's a habit . . . but,
my eyes are open.
I know where I am.
It is *my* fault.
I get out immediately.

CHAPTER FOUR

I walk down the same street.
There is a deep hole in the sidewalk.
I walk around it.

CHAPTER FIVE

I walk down another street.

WHAT IS A NO-WIN TRAP?
And How Does It Affect Your Life?

Your dilemma may seem utterly confounding and confusing, but there is actually a theory and a method to the madness that beleaguers you. Developing a working understanding of this theory can provide a way out of the maze and will help you avoid oncoming traps in the future.

When you feel you're caught up in a no-win situation, you are involved in what is often known as a "double bind." According to Webster's dictionary, a double bind is "a psychological predicament in which a person receives from a single source conflicting messages that allow no appropriate response to be made." In other words, you receive contradictory demands or expectations, so that any action taken is perceived to be wrong. The situation makes you feel you're up against a wall. A serious double bind can be so intense an experience that you feel the pressure right in your gut, as if you've just been stabbed.

Double-bind situations often build up slowly and catch you off guard. They can be subtle and insidious, wrapping you in a web of confusion. Most often, you don't recognize situations that have the potential to make you crazy until you're deeply involved and it's too late to escape. Then, even if you want to let go, you can't.

Without realizing it, a person may fall into a kind of "magical thinking" regarding double binds. It can seem easier to continue to try to improve a hopeless situation than to face the fact that you should let go.

The concept of the double bind has been of great interest to psychological theorists such as Bateson, Jackson, Haley, and Weakland, as described in *Steps to an Ecology of Mind*. Their research dealt with the connections between the complex double-bind communication patterns found in families with severe clinical issues, such as schizophrenia. The major point being made here is that whether or not we've dealt with these issues, in some way we *all* experience at least double binds sometime in our lives. Double binds have a way of invoking you to feel caught up in a never-ending torment of miscommunication. In varying degrees, you can find yourself feeling misunderstood, overwhelmed, undermined, minimized, humiliated, ostracized, or annihilated altogether. These feelings can be so discombobulating that many individuals find it almost easier to emotionally "numb out" and not feel much at all, thus invoking mental instabilities, personality distortions, and addictions.

This is not to say that your experience of double binds is literally going to make you crazy, only that your emotional perceptions and reactions may often resemble those with more serious and chronic mental disorders. Growing up in an environment of child abuse, addictions, and other severe dysfunction creates double-bind communication systems in families. Family members often feel trapped and frustrated, with no clear way out and no safe haven inside. It's not uncommon for those who have grown up under such conditions to develop a confused and confined perception of their role in relationships and in their interactions with the world. Even if you haven't grown up in a family with severe dysfunctions, it is easy to get entangled in conflicted expectations and communication cues with other family members, especially when difficult circumstances and major changes occur.

One of the ways this happens is that a pattern or precedent is set for "how things go and what part you play in them." You later find yourself—knowingly or unknowingly—seeking out similar situations, mostly because they feel familiar. While familiarity is not always healthy for us, the unconscious often confuses "that which we know" with "that which is safe." It is no coincidence that the words *family* and *familiar* share the same root.

The reason for considering issues and patterns of communication left over from your childhood is not to judge or condemn your parents or family, but to give insight into how you may have developed your ways of reacting or responding to life. If you can allow yourself to simply "watch the movie" of your past and glean what insights you can, you'll be more inclined to release yourself from the baggage of your past and move on to more positive and constructive ways of functioning. Examining past patterns of behavior will make it easier to steer clear of problems on the road ahead. The best way to escape no-win traps is to avoid falling into them to start with!

If, on the other hand, you fail to examine your problems objectively, and approach them instead with judgment and blame, you're bound to make everyone wrong, and you'll succeed only in prolonging your attachment to the no-win situation. It may also invite you to engage in new problematic attachments, believing you're justified in making even more individuals and groups entirely wrong. This no-win trap approach to life is incredibly debilitating and self-defeating: Your problems seem to multiply, growing overwhelmingly out of control.

The methods in this book focus on the basic "every day" double binds or no-win traps that everyone experiences one time or another—when you feel confronted or cornered to the point of believing you have no satisfactory or even workable way to turn. Consider the following conditions that are generally found in basic, though often painful and even excruciating, everyday no-win traps:

1. You feel trapped by a conflict or problem. You're convinced you can neither escape nor win the battle.

2. Despite this, you feel compelled or have a strong sense of responsibility to do something to solve the problem.

3. You believe you can't have a successful conversation with the person you need to talk to the most. That person is convinced the problem lies entirely with you, and approaching them only seems to make matters worse.

All three parts are crazy makers: You can drive yourself nuts trying to fix an unfixable problem.

Here are some questions to ask yourself to see if you're in a double bind now. They are also good questions to ask when you begin new relationships. They may lead you to alter the course of your involvement, take another route, or back out if necessary.

- Are you going round and round on the same issues with someone?

- Are you in the trap of not knowing what to do about the problem, but feel at the same time that you must do something or you'll feel guilty?

- Are others telling you what you should be doing, while you feel frozen, unable to move?

- Do you think that if you seek your own happiness or look out for yourself, you're selfish? Or do you believe that if you take care of yourself, you'll lose someone or something you feel you can't live without?

- Are you throwing up your hands and saying, "This is my lot in life. There's nothing I can do about it?"

- Do you feel someone or something else could save the day, even though no apparent solution appears to work?

- Do you feel that others who are involved in the situation desire a solution, or are they looking for a person to blame? If they do want to blame someone, could that person be you?

The more you answered yes to these questions, the more firmly you're stuck in a no-win trap. It's important to note here that the more you feel stuck—believing you have to continue playing the situation out the way you have been—the more likely it is that the solution to the problem lies with you. This point is not about blame, criticism, or putting you down. In fact, it's quite the opposite. It is with respect and regard for how difficult your situation is to you right now. It's quite possible that you're acting out of habit or a need to see yourself and/or others in a way that isn't entirely true or healthy for you.

Insight and practice will help you work out your own no-win situations. To begin that process, take a look at the following double-bind dilemma and ask yourself these questions: How would you respond? What steps would you take to get yourself out of the quicksand?

Feeling Stuck in Everyday Interactions

Picture yourself in an uncomfortable situation with a person you are deeply attached to on some level. This person might be a friend, a lover, or a business associate. The relationship began well but is beginning to sour.

At first you cared for this person, but lately you feel put down and annoyed. There's too much tension; you feel frustrated. Somewhere along the line, the relationship became unbalanced. You feel like you gave your power away, but when you think about it, there was actually an imbalance of power from the start.

Up until now, you didn't want to jeopardize the relationship, so you never considered evaluating your interaction with this person. You felt you had too much invested to rock the boat or make drastic changes, because the risk would be too great.

Now, if the relationship is with your boss or a coworker, the complications could affect your livelihood. And the old saying, "Think twice about rocking the boat if it isn't yours to rock," is running through your mind.

You may feel as though you aren't being respected in this relationship. Increasingly it seems that you never say the right thing or come up with the right answer. Inside, you are angry, and you take your anger out on other people. You may not even be fully aware of all this.

Finally, you come to the conclusion that you have to let this person know how you feel. But when the time comes, you say nothing. The chattering monkeys start with: "I'll distance myself . . . I'll be less available to him . . . maybe I'll switch departments." The tension is mounting. On the one hand, you are increasingly uptight about the situation, but on the other, you can't bring yourself to confront this growing problem. Your stomach churns when you picture how this person is going to react to your comments and concerns.

The no-win trap is before you. You're in a double bind. The crazy-making has begun. By now you're mumbling to yourself, "This dilemma is driving me crazy. I feel helpless. I don't know what to do, but I feel I should have control over it."

CATCH 22: ALLURING ASPECTS OF A DOUBLE BIND
Why You Take the Bait in a No-Win Trap

Considering how painful no-win traps are, you may be wondering why you're so often in one. Give yourself credit. There are some alluring if confounding reasons why double-bind scenarios attract so many and keep them invested in such painful situations. Consider the following:

- *You believe a great deal is at stake.* You don't want to lose the investment of whatever you've already put in. This is possibly what brought you to this harrowing point in the first place. Unfortunately, you could be confusing a "big investment" with the fact that you've invested in a fantasy of your own more than a reality, where everyone has a common goal. You'll probably get more satisfaction if you cut your losses and start over with a person or situation that is already going more in your direction. The problem is that you may not believe the world has anything better to offer you. See if you relate: "Even though he isn't very good to me, he's still the best man I've ever known!"

- *The pain seems worth the game.* You believe you have to endure this amount of pain in order to get what you want. Or maybe you're getting crumbs out of the whole deal, but you keep thinking it will one day turn into a piece of cake, if only you hang in there long enough. While your situation may not look appealing, it still seems better than other options or what you've experienced in the past. Consider the possibility that you don't realize you don't have to suffer to "get the good stuff." See if you relate: "When he and I are alone together, it's the best thing I've ever experienced. But the pain is so great when he goes for weeks without even calling."

- *You place your hopes or the "benefit of the doubt" in the wrong place.* It's important to acknowledge that there really are people who can talk an incredibly good game. So if you've been taken by a real good talker or a flimflammer, learn everything you can from the experience and pick yourself up and keep walking. However, it is up to you to be honest with yourself and listen to your inner voice if something doesn't sound quite right. If you've noticed all along that something didn't really ring true, and yet after all this time and disappointment you still believe there is a chance the other party will change if only you try harder, you could unfortunately be a magnet for being taken and getting stuck in perpetual no-win traps. The truth of the matter is that no one could get this person or situation to turn around, but you never consider that. See if you can relate: "He keeps on promising that his divorce is just around the corner. He sounds so sincere, it's just got to be true!"

- *You consider everyone else's needs and neglect your own.* Perhaps you are under the illusion that if you keep giving your all, those who have taken you for granted in the past will somehow begin to appreciate you and reciprocate with their kind giving. The reality could be that since you never directly express what you need, it never occurs to others that you even have any needs. Then, when you finally do get angry and say, "Look how much I've done for you and you never appreciate me!" others act surprised.

All of these are "lures" that keep us locked in a no-win trap. They're part of the mind games we play with ourselves. If we were truly observant and honest with ourselves, we'd be astounded by how much more we deceive ourselves than anyone else does. This false tale we tell ourselves regarding human relations is the thing that most binds us to the no-win trap. J. R. Pope wasn't kidding when he said, "Oh, what a tangled web we weave when first we practice to deceive."

We often run our lives as the sailors did in Greek mythology, lured into a terrible trap by the beautiful Sirens' song. We're driven to find out how much honey we can get without being stung by the bee, or how much hell we can cause and still get into heaven. What we fail to realize is that life has plenty of honey for us, without the jeopardy of the bee sting—if only we thought enough of ourselves to hold out for what's good for us.

Unfortunately, we often take what we get because it's all we think there is for us.

Irene Gets Engaged to Her "Ideal" Man

Irene wasn't looking for anyone new. In fact, she had just broken up with someone after two years of ongoing disappointment. She finally realized this man was more committed to making sure no relationship would ever work for him than finding one that would.

After kicking herself for not listening to her girlfriends and other well-meaning relationship advisers at work, Irene decided to give up on men completely. In fact, she made a pact with herself to only have men as friends.

Not long after making this inner contract with herself, Irene began having lunch almost daily with Jim, a male coworker who also resigned himself to never being able to find the love of his life. There was, however, one small difference between the two of them: Irene was single and Jim was married.

At the time, this arrangement seemed fine, as Irene saw him "only as a friend." Besides, she felt totally in charge of her feelings for Jim. She believed she'd successfully resigned herself to the "fact" that there are no good men out there. She promised herself—as if it was a good idea—that she would never lose control and take a chance on love again.

Irene told herself (and anyone who would listen), "I have come to see I am my own best friend, and I am fully complete myself." This statement would have been fine if it were true, but Irene unconsciously used it to make it appear as if she had it all together, when in reality she was still sore about her last fiasco, was licking her wounds and caught up in denial. Nevertheless, carrying this statement as a kind of banner for "renewal and newly found independence," she continued to meet Jim for lunch. Every day they commiserated on how tough relationships are.

Lo and behold, as time went on, their own lunchtime relationship developed into a personal and intimate one. They both came to the conclusion that it would be wise to have lunch as far from the office as possible in order to keep their budding relationship to themselves. Irene prided herself on how well she and Jim stuck with this idea. They kept their secret and no one knew.

Irene saw this as a tribute of Jim's commitment and concern for her, and Jim probably saw this as a good idea for him from any angle. Irene couldn't get over how easy Jim was to talk to. Over time, Jim found Irene to be the ideal woman he had always been seeking, and before long he promised her that he'd eventually leave his wife and become engaged to her.

When Irene finally confided this to her friends, they could barely believe what they were hearing, and raised the obvious questions. But Irene had a comeback for every objection: "Jim," she would say, "is different."

As the months went by and Jim assured Irene the divorce process was underway, Irene committed herself to getting promoted at work, along with getting married to Jim when the time was right. In fact, on Christmas that year, Jim gave her an engagement ring and promised that he would be divorced by April.

Well, April came and went. Not only had Jim not divorced the bane of his existence, but he was also assigned to Irene's department. Irene remembers it well. On May 16, after having an explosive fight with Jim at a park all too near their office, she received word from her boss that Jim was now assigned to work directly for her. The memo on her desk also explained that his evaluation was up for review in two weeks.

Upon reading this, Irene took her "engagement ring" off and threw it against the bulletin board over her desk. Frantically forgetting where she was, she yelled out for anyone to hear, "I can't believe I did it again! What was I thinking?"

Can you relate to any of this? If so, don't think you're alone. So many of us get ourselves into situations that seem so "right" at the time, but are just one more cover-up in a long line of self-deceptions. If you can, be kind to yourself. You're only human. But you must try to realize that the more you're willing to look at yourself honestly and let go of ideas that don't serve you, the easier it will be for you to change and escape your no-win trap.

BECOME MORE AWARE OF YOUR FEELINGS

One way to begin the process of avoiding the double bind is to become aware of those feelings in your life that might lure you to seeing the "attractive" side of a potential no-win situation. This requires strength and diligence. We must always keep an eye out for the deceptive bait of a no-win trap. How many of the following are inclined to get you?

1. *Loneliness.* Few other feelings in life can lead us into joining up with the wrong company as much as this one.

2. *Hurt.* We'll often take on companionship with a vengeance as a way to help us lick our wounds.

3. *Anger.* A sense of self-righteous justification can lead us to believe that doing the wrong thing is the right way to get back at someone. It's good to remember the old proverb, "Being

kind in the midst of an angry moment will save you 100 days of sorrow." If seeing red doesn't allow you the luxury of kindness, perhaps your mantra should be something like: "The best revenge is good living."

4. *Fear.*   The fear of never having enough money, or of not having the career you want or the love you need, can drive you to take whatever comes along because you think there will be nothing else available for you. Not believing the world or universe would ever "conspire in your favor" is one reason people settle for a handful of crumbs, or stay in a hellish situation. They believe it's the only option.

   Other fears are worse. Fear of rejection and fear of abandonment are the strongest lures of the no-win trap. If you're afraid of being left out in the cold, of being tossed out by your family, or of losing your ability to survive, you're bound to find yourself in places you truly do not want to be. Sometimes it's a matter of staying in these situations until you're prepared to survive on your own. If you end it before you're sufficiently ready, you could find yourself returning with your tail between your legs, subjecting yourself to treatment even worse than before.

5. *Convenience.*   A man once told me he continued to sleep with his wife, whom he recently had divorced, because she continued to make herself available to him. When I told him that didn't sound like a winning idea, he acted surprised. Accepting something just because it's easy and available is a surefire way to tell the universe you really aren't counting on much this time around.

HAUNTING FAMILIARITIES

People and patterns familiar from our past often haunt present situations in our lives. Consider the following lines that people often use:

"I don't get it. I can't live with him, and I can't live without him."

"Even my mother didn't treat me as badly as you do."

"How come I always date the same people?"

One of the subtler lures of the recurrent no-win trap is related to the process of healing. We're all driven in part by an unconscious desire to heal the wounds of childhood. Too often this leads us to repeat old patterns of behavior in order to finally "master" them. The only way to actually master them, of course, is to become aware of their influence in our lives and to consciously avoid the traps they present.

We are often drawn into difficult, no-win situations because they force us to have compassion for parents and others whom we feel have slighted or hurt us in some way. Failing that, however, we may miss the lesson of forgiveness, and disdain them until the day they die (and even after). It often seems we take on intolerable relationships and situations to prove our parents wrong, or to fix our past in some way. But we soon find ourselves in over our heads, to the point of wondering how we'll ever get out.

All of these pitfalls are largely the products of our minds and our pasts, our personal contributions to the no-win trap. Unfortunately, it doesn't stop there. Life can throw us curveballs entirely on its own. So keep reading: Having gotten this far into Chapter 1, you're probably already on your way to looking at yourself and your true motivations more honestly. That's a huge first step, and a sign that a solution is near.

THREE TYPES OF NO-WIN TRAPS

While life conditions present us with all sorts of double binds, they all tend to fit into one of the following three main categories:

- Situational no-win traps

- Interpersonal no-win traps

- Circuit overload no-win traps

Often, one of these traps can lead to another, and you find your situation developing into a combination of two traps, or even all three.

Situational no-win traps often involve having simultaneous needs or goals that conflict. If you're unable to be assertive and direct about delegating responsibility or asking for what you need, these traps can often lead into interpersonal no-win traps. If the interpersonal problems continue to go unaddressed, too many things can go wrong at once, paralyzing you in a circuit overload no-win trap.

In the following sections, I'll discuss these types in more detail. Each discussion will consider a place for you to begin taking action toward finding more relief in your life, and consequently lightening your burdens.

Situational No-Win Traps

Situational no-win traps involve a change in circumstance. They generally arise with a change in some significant aspect of your life: job status, marital status, income level, and so on. They are further compounded with ongoing needs or responsibilities. This often presents you with conflicting goals, which you feel required to satisfy simultaneously, as unrealistic as that might be.

Any transition in these areas carries with it a potential for chaos. While change is often a great chance for growth and opportunity, it's often accompanied by unknowns and downsides you don't envision. This can be true even when the change is intentional and seemingly under your control.

When going through a change in your life, the more you are on the lookout for hazards that may arise, the more you can be prepared when they finally do occur. This involves being equally aware of *your own reaction*—the way you typically respond to change—in order not to add to the problem if a double bind begins to occur.

The following are several types of situational changes that could throw you into an unexpected no-win trap. As you read them, consider how you've reacted in the past and how you might respond in the future.

- You recently got the promotion of a lifetime at work. It will require much travel and time away from home. However, you also just promised your wife you would spend more time with her and the kids.

- You're late for an important meeting and realize you're driving 85 mph on the freeway. You've already gotten two speeding tickets this year, trying to fit too many meetings into one day. You can't afford to get another one. You also can't miss this meeting or you'll lose your job. You knew your promotion would mean more work for you, but you didn't realize it would come to this.

- You have a teenage daughter who lives with you half the time. You just found out you landed a job you always wanted, and it requires you to be out of the country a lot of the time. While you know you won't have your daughter with you for many more years, you don't know if this job opportunity will come back around again either.

- The judge awards you 50 percent custody of your two kids after a drawn-out court battle. A week later your corporation downsizes and tells you the only way you can keep your job and its benefits for your children is to relocate out of state. Unfortunately, moving the children is not an option in the divorce.

- Your hours as a flight attendant were drastically shortened by cutbacks. To make up for lost income, you find a part-time position that could lead into the career you've always wanted. However, it interferes with the minimal flight schedule you do have. You consider leaving your flying career, but you don't want to lose the benefits you have.

- You've met the love of your life, and you've finally got your career off the ground. You didn't realize how much time and effort they would both require. Not wanting to give up either of them, you find yourself exhausted most of the time.

The first and most important step in dealing with these seemingly intractable no-win situations is to keep them from spiraling into the overly emotional interpersonal realm. As much as possible, try treating these dilemmas as specific challenges to work through, rather than seeing them as bad karma or unfortunate luck. Think of them as strategically designed to help you determine what is *really* important in your life. You'll be inclined to get through them much quicker if you don't blow them out of proportion.

As we discussed earlier, one of the basic conditions for a double bind is that you believe you can't have a successful conversation with the person you need to talk to the most. While this may seem an insurmountable obstacle, there are ways you might be able to bring the issue up for discussion without completely antagonizing the other party.

The best way to do this is to first work through your own feelings and beliefs about the dilemma before you, and then take them to the other person. To help you with this process, carefully consider the following ideas. They can help you work on your issues by isolating each section of the problem. Separating aggravating parts from the whole can allow you to see the forest from the trees and keep you from becoming overwhelmed. If you find after these steps are taken that you still can't talk about it, then it's likely that the double bind you're dealing with has the complexities of an interpersonal no-win trap, which we'll discuss later on in this chapter and throughout the rest of the book.

- *Write down each part of your situational no-win trap.* Maybe there's more involved in this circumstance than you realize. The simple act of writing down your thoughts and feelings can help you to view them more objectively. Think of yourself as a paid consultant on the matter. The more you're able to detach yourself from the issues, the more they'll simply be problems to be solved rather than monsters that will defeat and destroy you.

- *Make a list of pros and cons.* Determine which option will provide the most advantage for you, and what's important in the long run. Don't forget to consider contingencies.

- *Deal with the vacillation in your mind.* There's nothing more overwhelming than bouncing back and forth between which decisions to make. If you find your thoughts go around and around in your mind, or if you're waking up in the middle of the night, consider taking steps to lower your stress (see the "Chattering Monkeys" exercise in Chapter 7). This will help you come to a decision more effectively.

- *Don't assume there's no room for negotiation with the other parties involved if you haven't tried.* Concerning situational double binds, it's important to get as much information as possible before determining what issues the situation has for you. Find out what is actually expected of you and where everyone else stands. People will be more inclined to listen to your point of view when your evident well-being makes you more effective in whatever you're doing with them.

What separates a situational double bind from an interpersonal one is that the situation itself is more what binds you than the personalities of the people involved. The more you're able to have successful communication about the situation with the premise that you're all working on solving a problem together, the less it will fall into the emotional realm, where interpersonal no-win traps live.

Interpersonal No-Win Traps

These traps are more emotionally involved than the situational traps we just discussed. They also have the added complexities of difficult or impossible communication.

While situational double binds can get complicated due to matters of the heart, interpersonal double binds involve circumstances in which you are technically free to detach yourself at any time, but there is some inner need that keeps you tied to the turbulence—often as if your life depended on it. Interpersonal double binds can appear to be about what's going on with the other party, but when you look more closely at the underpinnings of the conflict, the story is more about you.

How deeply entrenched your interpersonal double bind becomes depends on how strongly you feel you have the right to have your needs met. Take a look at the following case scenarios. Ask yourself if you would pull out sooner rather than later.

- The man of your dreams has finally proposed to you. The hitch is, as he asked for your hand, he disclosed that he has continued illegally using drugs behind your back. You love this man with all your heart and want to spend the rest of your life with him. However, you also recognize the reality of trying to be a one-woman detox center. Part of you wants to stay and see him through, and the other part wants to run the other way. What would you do?

- While your new husband does seem to have more control over your son's temper tantrums than you ever did, you feel he goes too far when he disciplines him. When you bring this up, he says, "Someone has to be on top of this." As time goes on, you become more and more frightened that your son—and you—could be physically abused.

- You graduated from law school and are firmly entrenched in your career. You took what you thought was the job opportunity of a lifetime. However, five years into the practice, after receiving the best cases in the firm, you realize that you're not sure you can live with the business dealings of the senior partners and your colleagues. In fact, the more you see, the more you're afraid of getting sued yourself. One day, the retiring senior partner comes into your office and says, "We are so pleased with your work, we would like to make you a partner of our firm and help see me into my retirement." What do you do?

- Your best friend recently got a promotion and is now your supervisor. Since then, she hardly talks to you personally anymore. To make matters worse, none of the other coworkers confide in you, fearing you'll tell your friend. You resent being alone and, with nowhere to turn, feel stuck.

- Your divorce has been finalized for a year and a half. You begin dating a woman whom you like very much, but you aren't sure you want to get married. She insists that if she's going to continue seeing you, you'll at least have to introduce her to your kids. However, you don't want the children to get involved in case she isn't going to be "the one."

Each one of these scenarios has a better chance of a happy ending— at least for you—if you feel you're in a position of equal footing, or of having the right to be heard and your needs met. If you don't believe that's the case, it's important to recognize you're at a fork in the road. Interpersonal no-win traps arise when our own self-esteem is at stake, when we're not sure our needs can or even deserve to be met. Among other things, this book is about helping you find your self-esteem and to recognize that without it, life is only one double bind after another.

Let's now move to the next level of the no-win trap, to those situations that often force us to grow despite ourselves. When things become unbearable, there's nothing left but to stop and say, "Enough! I can't take anymore! Something has to change!"

Circuit Overload No-Win Traps

These traps compound the nightmare of the two types of double binds mentioned above. Circuit overloads occur when you're barraged with too many pressures coming all at once, when it's nearly impossible to figure out what to deal with first. The bad news is, this can be so overwhelming you wonder how you can possibly survive. The good news is, this is the situation your soul might have been waiting for. Perhaps you needed to get this deeply into trouble in order to find out who you really are.

- You're living with relatives while attending college, and one of them loses his job. Now they're asking you to help out with even more bills than you already were. As the days and weeks go on, you have to work more hours at your part-time job to help out with the family, and your grades are getting lower. One day, the pressure is so heavy, you feel like you're about to collapse. Whose needs should you be taking care of and what will you do now?

- While your ex-husband pays you child support and some alimony, you find you still have to work two jobs to pay all the unexpected bills you had been incurring since your divorce. After two years of this, and buying a house for you and your children, your oldest child complains that you're never home. He threatens to move back in with Dad. One afternoon, after hearing this litany one time too many, you drive off in a huff and total your car.

- Your father has died and your mother is afraid to be alone. The rest of the family is not involved, and she tells you that you're the only person she has left in her life. In fact, leaning on you has been her lifetime preoccupation. After visiting your mother every day for two weeks and taking time off from work, you realize you need to bring outside resources into the situation to help. As you mention to your mom that you cannot do this alone, she goes into hysterics and cries, "You're the only person I can trust."

Quite often, a situation or relationship can at first seem simple to the naked eye. What you see at first, however, is rarely what you ultimately get. Changing situations and new information tend to complicate matters. Aspects you overlook become problems you never predicted. Soon things can snowball into a full-blown circuit overload no-win trap.

Using the three categories of no-win traps makes it easier to gain insight into the true nature of your problem, and helps to clarify what strategies are required to set things right. As mentioned before, there are some dilemmas that incorporate all three no-win traps into one. You'll eventually discover, however, that in just about every instance one of the types of double binds will upset you more than the others. That will be the one to focus on so you can isolate where to put your energy, and not become distracted by all the different aspects of the problem. Each type of trap is potentially chaotic and must be handled in its own way.

The only thing more important than knowing the game you're playing is keeping your eye on the ball. When we feel ambushed or blind-sided by others, more often than not it's our own eyes that have deceived us. It is truly amazing how spending a simple day at the races with someone can turn into being married to a full-blown gambling addict!

There is good news, however. Hardly any of this happens overnight. There are stages and phases in the building of a relationship with another person, with a job, and with any other important aspect of your life. What's key to remember in all of these is that the most important relationship you'll ever have is the one you have with yourself.

2

The Birth of a No-Win Trap

The minute you settle for less than you deserve, you get even less than you settled for.

Maureen Dowd

*N*o-win traps, like any other development of human nature gone awry, do not happen overnight. They take time and have several stages. In this chapter we'll explore the very beginning of those stages, examining just how double binds get started and begin to work their way into the fabric of your mind. You'll learn how to identify ingredients of a double bind and how yours might have gotten started. Then you can begin to take a look at how you might get out. By understanding where the traps begin, you'll come to feel more like an insider, plotting the story of your life. Rather than feeling like a victim of circumstances beyond your control, you'll come to see how you are both the creator and director of the play that is your life.

> *When you see how you've cast yourself in negative roles with yourself and others, you'll learn how to "recast" yourself in positive roles and to avoid negative roles in the future.*

Rather than trying to please everybody else, you'll learn how to take better care of yourself. It's a matter of recognizing when you have a reasonable chance of succeeding with your present modus operandi, when to alter your course, and when you'd do better to step out altogether.

Choosing positive roles doesn't mean others won't cast you in negative ones. It means you won't buy into their false belief about you. It means you will steadfastly hold to who you really are.

It's a matter of realizing that you can get what you want in life with less pain, if any, and to be realistic about what to expect in the situation you're currently in. It's a matter of seeing how you set yourself up for disappointment when you insist on accepting crumbs as meals. It means being able to live with yourself even if others won't.

Of course, all this requires that you become more and more true to yourself. That, after all, is what this life's journey is all about.

Being true to yourself requires you to be truly honest and accountable with how you take in and respond to information and activity within and around you. The more you can observe the goings-on in life as an ongoing flow of activity that allows for your responsible *choice* of how involved or uninvolved you will be with any of it and what part, if any, you will play, the more you can regulate to a large degree how much peace or how much chaotic drama you will have in your life. The more you think you have to jump into the frey of whatever is going on with no discretion or forethought about it, the more your life is in the hands of others, and you could be set up for taking what is left at the bottom of the barrel in almost any situation.

We often take less than ideal positions on the game board of life, as if there were no other places to lay down our chips. The reality is, we can change the positions we play by changing *who we are* in the game. That's the secret, really: what *you* believe you really are.

HOW DO WE CREATE A NO-WIN TRAP?

There's a recipe to making a double bind, much like cooking an unhealthy meal. The ingredients are made up of negative conversations we knowingly and unknowingly have in our heads. These inner conversations are often derived from what we assume others think of us, along with pressures or obsessions that plague our minds and keep us from following our better judgment.

In fact, I believe we all have our own good judgment. It's just that somewhere along the way, we allow others to persuade us not to use it, as if they somehow know what's best for us. In a moment we'll take a look at some "ingredients" that may have set you up for a double bind. If you can better understand what went into the stew you're in, you'll have a better chance of changing the recipe and cooking something better for yourself.

Consider exploring these "no-win trap inducers," not as fuel for engaging in anger and hurt, but simply as insights into the nature of your double binds. Before going forward, here's a helpful hint to aid you in this process:

> *Learning* from your past helps you to let it go. It frees you from all sorts of traps and binds.

> *Judging* the past ensures that you'll be stuck in it forever.

NO-WIN TRAP INDUCER I
Expecting More Than People Can Give

The first and main ingredient of a double bind goes all the way back to our childhood. It's the belief that because someone is in a position of friendship, parenting, love and/or authority in our lives, they always do and say things for *our* own good. Either that, or they should, without having any major needs or unfinished business of their own.

In reality, many who've been given rights, responsibilities, and authority are pretty lousy at their jobs and should never have been put in a position of influence over children. Nevertheless, it happens all the time. And when we experience unhealthy behaviors in our role models, we can easily believe that their behaviors are actually okay. We can even begin to believe that they were actually doing the right thing, and that if we felt something was wrong, it was most likely something that was wrong with us.

The no-win trap arises later, when, as adults, we go out into the world and recruit others to be in our lives who are just like these caregivers from our childhood. We do this since we are generally magnetized to what is familiar. Even if we're consciously determined to avoid dating someone who isn't anything like dear old Dad, it is uncanny what often happens. Months or years later, you can find yourself screaming at the top of your lungs to someone whom you thought would be different, "You're just like my father!"

There appears to be some sort of primal mandate deeply embedded within the wisdom of our souls to make some sense or peace with what has come before us and happened early on. When we conduct our lives without "knowing" this, and are overly fueled and blinded with judgment and blame, we're inevitably disappointed, and wonder in bewilderment where our lives went "wrong."

Once we're locked in this no-win trap, we tend to wait forever for this imperfect soul we've chosen to be with to finally change and measure up to our standards. Either that or we attempt to change ourselves, endlessly trying to please the "unpleasable." Eventually, we come to either hate the other person because he or she couldn't be what we wanted them to be, or we hate ourselves for not being able to be what they wanted us to be. Often, we do both. This misconceived and exhausting process is one of the most intractable double binds of all.

In the case below, it is the perception of a girl's relationship with her parents that originally gave rise to the no-win trap. People who insist on either beating up on their parents or making them into saints are inclined to become victims who fail to take responsibility for themselves. They're also inclined to double-bind others, making them pay for their parents' perceived failures.

Marilyn Doesn't Go to Juilliard

Marilyn was one of the prettiest girls in her high school, and could sing better than anyone else in the school. She grew up on a farm in the Midwest and was her father's pride and joy. Everyone knew about Marilyn. She sang in school, at church, and in choir competitions clear across the Great Plains states. She had a sister, Evelyn, who was short and heavy and had no apparent talent other than winning her mother's favor no matter what Marilyn accomplished. (It never occurred to Marilyn at the time that one of the most "attractive" features about her sister, as far as Mom was concerned, was that she wasn't good at anything, and thus didn't intimidate her mother like the gifted Marilyn did.)

At any rate, Marilyn truly believed her mother wanted the best for her, and that if she only pleased her for once in some way, her mom would soften toward her and show the love she seemed to only show to Evelyn. After all, Mom was perfect. Aren't they all?

By the time Marilyn reached her junior year in high school and was looking into colleges, she was inspired by her dad to apply to music schools all over the country. Thanks to him, she'd had many years of serious musical and singing training. Her father also had a strong musical background and at one time had been a musician himself, before he married, returned to his hometown, and took over his uncle's farm. Marilyn loved to listen to Dad's stories about all the fun he had in his twenties, traveling around the country playing the trumpet for Broadway shows.

When Marilyn received an invitation to interview at the famed Juilliard School of Music in New York she told her parents she wanted to go. Her mother hit her with a line that has echoed in her ears forever: "Only girls looking for trouble would ever go to New York." While her father was thrilled, his genuine concern for Marilyn's safety led him to agree with her mother. In fact, he even went into a whole rendition about the time he was held up outside Carnegie Hall.

Hiding her disappointment, Marilyn agreed not to go. Instead she went to her state university, where she certainly got a fine education, and eventually became a music teacher. But she didn't become the opera singer she had always wanted to be.

After college, Marilyn married a man who had gone to the same college, and they both taught at the same high school. While she loved Bill, Marilyn never seemed to get Mom's blessing. He wasn't exactly her dreamboat either, but she thought marrying a nice man would please her mother.

As the years went by and she raised two boys of her own, Marilyn grew tired of feeling she always had to settle for less. Even when it came to taking vacations, if she wanted to venture down to Mexico and stay in Manzanillo, Bill managed to talk her into going to the Texas coast instead.

Then, on Marilyn's fortieth birthday, when her mom came up with some reason why she wouldn't be able to come to her party and her dad came alone, it occurred to her that she would never be able to please good old mom, no matter what she did. Not long after blowing out the candles, while most of the guests were preoccupied with eating cake, she went out to the backyard and began to cry.

Her Aunt Susan, her mother's sister, came outside and put her arm around Marilyn as she wept like a baby. Susan always knew about the discord that existed between Marilyn and her mother. She also knew her sister had always been jealous of Marilyn. Trying to comfort her niece, Susan told her how proud of her she was and what a wonderful woman she'd grown up to be.

Marilyn continued to cry, and asked, "Then why does Mom hate me so much?"

Susan hugged her even harder and said, "Oh honey, don't you know? Your mother was always jealous of your dad's fondness for you and his passion for music. She was afraid that if you went to New York, he'd run off and go with you and leave her and Evelyn here."

Marilyn stared at her aunt, feeling even more crushed. All this time, she'd believed that if she could only be better or somehow more pleasing, her mother would let her into her heart. The truth, however, was that no matter what she ever did, she would *never* gain her mother's regard. She hadn't realized that she could change her perspective any time, especially as an adult.

From then on, Marilyn decided to turn a cold shoulder to the family she had grown up with, giving up on pleasing her mom and only seeing her father once in a while. She threw herself into leading her local choir and forced herself to act as if she couldn't be happier with her life and her husband, Bill. In reality, she was dying inside, and felt more and more bitter as the years went on.

Then one day, her choir got invited to perform with other church choirs around the country in New York City. Everyone was determined to go. Marilyn, however, insisted on sticking with the original story that New York was just too dangerous, "especially after 9/11 and all." She decided she would stay home, and sent the assistant director in her place. After all the years she'd spent avoiding her own dreams in hopes of winning her mother's love and attention, the only investment she had left in her life was punishing herself for not listening to her soul.

Marilyn decided to stay locked in her no-win trap. If she went to New York and had a great time, she would never be able to forgive herself for not going to Juilliard in the first place. If she didn't go, she would just never know, and could feel saintlike and better than Mom for "doing the right thing."

Marilyn had spent her life trying to get more love from her mother than her mother was able to give. That impossible quest led to the abandonment of Marilyn's own hopes and dreams, and locked her in a no-win trap of resentment and defeat. It is truly difficult to have the objective insight to recognize what a significant person in our lives, such as a parent or someone else with great authority, can or cannot give to us. It's also not easy to detect what their own inner needs and true motivations really are.

This is especially so when we're more focused on what we desperately want from them than on what they're actually doing. This is why developing a sense of discernment—being able to see clearly "what is," without judgment or blame, as early on in our lives as possible—is so important. When we fully understand what we need, and we're willing to go where that need can effectively be met, or are prepared to wait until we locate it, we have the best chance of staying out of no-win traps.

There are no traps quite like the ones we set for ourselves. What's amazing is how we use other people—our parents, siblings, spouses, children—along with time and money issues, to put a damper on who we are. We tell ourselves *they* hold us back. In reality, *we* hold ourselves back, because our own inner supportive voices aren't strong enough to hold their own over what we perceive we're being told by others.

In its own sad way, perhaps taking the "safer" route or telling herself she wanted to please her mom more than be herself, were noble excuses Marilyn's unconscious drummed up to prop up her angry and hurt ego: If she focused on blaming everyone else, she wouldn't have to face herself.

Somewhere beneath the surface, Marilyn's own doubts and fears about whether she could have "made it" in school at Juilliard, or the fear of being away from her family, may have unconsciously set her up to never find out how she would do. Perhaps she was afraid she'd disappoint her father and not measure up to him, or flunk out the first semester and have to come home with her tail between her legs and hear her mother say, "I told you so."

While Marilyn had much more going for her than her sister did, she did not have the internal "root love connection" with her mom that Evelyn did. The lack of that connection can lead a person to put their lifelong energy into trying to please a parent who cannot be pleased, rather than focusing on using the talents they have.

A no-win trap can occur anytime you drain yourself by putting more energy into pleasing someone else than your "self"—even a parent. This is not to confuse being small and "selfish" and only considering what you want in a self-absorbed way with your higher, true, or more authentic self. Many times, you can find yourself linked with family members who have "given up" who they really wanted to be in order to fit in with the perceived needs of the family. They can lead you to believe that you're selfish or self-centered, when you're actually being your true self, instead of falling into an old, negative family pattern. Rather than congratulating you for holding your own, you may even be shunned for having the audacity to be yourself.

It's helpful to remember that in some way all relationships are about self-love. They either:

- Help you love yourself more than you probably would on your own, if they elevate your heart and soul, or

- Teach you not to buy into what appears to be going on with the other party, because you know you're worth more than what they're dishing out about you.

NO-WIN TRAP INDUCER 2
Not Recognizing Entropy

Psychological entropy takes place when you're putting out greater amounts of energy to someone or some endeavor than you're getting back. There's an absence of balance and flow. You're the only one giving to the situation, while others are only taking. Over time, resentment builds. You begin to feel they're "getting away with murder."

The confusing part about this, which lends itself to no-win traps, is that quite often you do get good things from someone, but you feel there is also a price to pay for it. The higher your esteem and the better you feel about yourself, the more you'll come to see that you can get what you need without having to pay for it negatively.

This can happen at any point in your life, and in any number of different contexts. At home, you may be the only adult child in a family who takes care of Grandma. On the job, you may feel you're the only one doing the work, while everyone else is sliding by. In friendships, you may be the one who does all the listening while others do all the talking.

In these situations, you're bound to find yourself muttering, "Why don't I just leave this job [situation] or at least get some help?" Even though others may encourage you to do so, there's some kind of attraction or reinforcement that seems to keep you hanging in there. How long you continue depends on how much you're willing to put up with and how little you're willing to receive.

Jackie Plays the "Can You Top This" Game

The incident for Jackie occurred at a family barbeque hosted by her best-intentioned grandmother. For years, Jackie's family get-togethers had been battlefields of rivalry for Jackie, her sister Gwen, and her cousin Paul, while the senior members of the family looked on.

During this particular version of the "Can You Top This" game, Paul was in limbo with nothing much to report. Gwen had been going through some rough times so she was down a notch. Not Jackie, however. She was racing full speed ahead.

Wearing a flashy black and yellow, size-six dress, Jackie took center stage, cackling away about her two-year contract with a consulting group. Uncle Charles, oohing and ahhing while Jackie showed off her expensive four-color presentation folder, said, "Jackie, you are really in a position to make something of yourself here."

Frenetically moving around the crowd, Jackie relished her spotlight role in gaining the family's momentary attention with her recent accomplishment. Meanwhile, Gwen and Paul sat silently as Jackie blabbed away. During and after her performance, Paul never looked at her, and neither he nor Gwen offered their congratulations. And why should they? This threesome had been playing the "can you top this" game for years within the nuclear and extended family.

Shortly after achieving her few minutes of attention, Jackie and Gwen got ready to play a game of tennis. While everyone was walking toward the court, Jackie overheard her father tell Gwen, "I'll give you five bucks if you beat the hell out of her."

Months later, after Jackie had gone through an auto accident, a near divorce, and a bout of major depression, she realized her frantic moves to put her own dent in the planet were, in fact, ruining her life.

Isn't it amazing what you will go through just to gain a couple of minutes of attention or a few words of recognition? Perhaps you can relate to this saga of always struggling to outdo yourself. Maybe you, too, place demands on yourself that can put you over the edge.

NO-WIN TRAP INDUCER 3
Not Taking Care of Yourself

There is no stronger ingredient for a double bind than continuing to live, act, and think like a dependent child, especially when you *pretend* to be an evolved and enlightened human being. You're only fooling yourself. An unwillingness to make a commitment to taking full responsibility for your own actions and welfare leaves you vulnerable to the whims and agendas of others. This can lead to dependent relationships and lowering your self-esteem. I know this well—I've been through it. In fact, when it comes to self-responsibility, I'm continuing to grow and face myself every day.

Without consciously realizing it, I was living on the hope that someday a kind male creature would eventually show up and save me from myself. This unrecognized fantasy was left over from some inner Cinderella tape that kept running through my mind on its own power, long after the childhood batteries had gone dead.

Having left a severely unhappy marriage and struck out on my own, I believed I'd already taken the steps to make me responsible for myself. But just because I'd left a marriage that was killing me didn't mean I was *committed* to being an independent adult in my soul.

Over time, as much as I was thankful that I was no longer in an unhappy marriage, the continuing struggle to pull myself through life had gotten rough. Tired of all the "trying to find myself routine, I fell into yet one more no-win trap with another incompatible man. He "happened" to have an MD. You'd think I would have gotten it. But evidently, the story in my head, which I'd heard from my mother since birth—"Marry a doctor; you'll never have to worry"—was still floating around in my brain like an insatiable tapeworm.

Thankfully, I recouped more quickly this time, and was thankful that I'd gotten out before the relationship was too far along. In rethinking what I'd done, I realized it was a last-ditch effort of sorts to see if I could find a way to be "happy," by leaning on someone who I *thought* would be able to manage money and life better than I could.

I had internalized the idea that it actually takes less effort to grow up and embrace becoming a responsible adult than it does to hide behind someone's coattails and never be who you really are. And now I finally got it. True responsibility is not a burden. When done authentically, it's about being able to respond effectively to life. Being responsible, and not blaming others or yourself for your own misgivings, gives you the freedom to make choices and decisions from a position of having true options, instead of desperately running from one needy situation to another.

It's important to remember the saying, "She who waits for her knight will have to clean up after his horse." We may get the man we think we want, only to end up with a mess. The maiden needs to be responsible and discerning in choosing her knight. It's not like choosing a dress. When you walk into the store, at least you have some idea what size you are. When you meet the potential love of your life, however, the only knowledge you usually have is how painful your loneliness is. Hardly the best way to take the measure of a man. We generally end up taking home the first one that's halfway decent. If women put as much energy into picking out the groom as they do buying the dress and the wedding cake, we'd have a lot more long-term marriages.

Of course, all of this is true for men as well as for women, and it also applies to more than just our intimate relationships. We often choose our jobs, friends, attorneys, and interior decorators the same way. We jump in too soon.

Our problem, clearly, is not the people we choose to be with, but the eyes we use to pick them out. We're dazzled by the shining armor or the stunning face and figure, and disappointed when we finally find the real person hidden inside. In fact, the sad part is, we're often dazzled by a whole lot less than that. Quite often we'll fall for anyone who gives us a second look and treats us a little better than whoever we were with during the last fiasco.

If you think that the man of your dreams is going to help you hide out from yourself, or the woman of your fantasies will live up to your hype or hers, you're stepping into a no-win trap right from the start. Besides, anyone who is willing to do that for you will surely have some unsavory price for you to pay in return, which usually includes covering up for their misgivings in some way.

On the other side of the coin, a no-win situation is waiting for anyone who confuses a "challenge" with someone who has more problems than the Betty Ford Center could manage. While women certainly fall into this category, men are even more prone to falling for the "Mighty Mouse Syndrome." They think they can take on your problems and save you from certain disaster.

A good rule to follow is to not even consider dating someone if you don't think they have an 85 percent or higher chance of living positively and taking intelligent advice. You might be saying, "Gee, that rules a lot of people out." But that's just the problem. People who tend to get disappointed have low standards at the start.

We immediately fall into the lion's den when we settle for less in the beginning, and blame the other person for deceiving us in the end. The truth is, you always get what you ask for if you're willing to *wait* for what you want, and clean up your own self and behavior in the meantime. The problem is, you're afraid that will never happen, so you take the first person who appears somewhat tolerable, and you try to make them into what you wanted in the first place.

It's amazing how we still refuse to believe that "you can't turn a sow's ear into a silk purse" actually applies to people. The best way to begin to correct the habit of trying to disprove this bit of wisdom is to at least get out as soon as you know something really isn't working. Don't deceive yourself further while pompously pretending you're "giving them the benefit of the doubt." The only "benefit" that's going on when this tape is running through your head is that you're prolonging the inevitability of having to face and then clean up yet one more disaster.

To see if you're inclined to get caught up in a dependency double bind, here are a few questions to ask yourself:

- Do you often make yourself responsible for other people while leaving your own needs for last?

- Are you living your life right now in such a way that you could continue to do so if no one else came along to help you out in the future?

- Do you find yourself mainly glad you're with someone because they take care of important tasks that you would never want to be responsible for yourself? Or do you have a way of setting others up to be the "designated driver" in your life and clean up after your messes because you can't handle difficult or even everyday situations, such as responsibly paying bills, making phone calls for doctor's appointments, dealing with the IRS, or calling the police when you get into a car accident?

- Do you tell someone not to act like your mother or father, but set him or her up to be that way by your irresponsible or addictive behavior?

- Are you "as good" as the people you want to be with?

- Are things so bad you would be willing to put up with almost anything if someone came to bail you out?

- Are you afraid you'd lose the one you "love" if they were able to take care of themselves?

- Are you able to responsibly ask for help and actually make use of it when the need arises?

- Does the person you're with inspire you to be a better person, or are you preoccupied with feeling you deserve better? Are you already evolving into a better person, or do you require constant cheerleading from others in order to get through the day?

The less you're willing to take responsibility for yourself, the more likely you are to fall into a no-win trap. It's important to remember that every relationship and every situation starts out where the last one left off. If you recently took a job willy-nilly, just to get out of a horrible situation, be prepared to find the same problem—in a different suit—passing you in the hall. Any lesson you haven't learned will come upon you again. Unfinished business and unfinished growing always catch up with us. The best way to stay out of ongoing trouble is to face what you're avoiding in your life and deal with what's inside.

Enough said. There's no fun like the fun you have as a responsible adult who is willing and able to manage themselves honestly, every day. There's no no-win trap like the one you end up in when you refuse to grow up and be an adult.

NO-WIN TRAP INDUCER 4
Not Getting Help When You Need It

Don't confuse dependency with asking for help when you need it. We all need outside help at some point in our lives; being self-responsible includes knowing when and how to get that help.

The "when" here is very important. It's better to deal with the issues you have sooner rather than later. If you let everything pile up, and some unexpected situation occurs, you can be left hanging with very few options. This leaves you more vulnerable to get caught up again in another no-win trap. Those who keep putting off asking for help are most likely to find themselves devastated when a major life trauma hits and they have no one to go to. They'll end up trying to get help too late from someone who'll fail to come through for them, thus reinforcing their belief that no one's there when you need them.

If you ask for help when you're still standing on your own two feet, when you're able to understand the positive flow of give and take, you're more likely to engage healthy people who can give the honest help you need. If you wait until you're sinking, your desperation will attract those who may have their own agendas and needs, people more likely to use or hurt you in some way.

If you have unmet needs, don't put off addressing them. You don't want to be one of those people who walk around acting strong and arrogant, claiming to have everything under control, when in reality they're simply too afraid to let others know how much help they need.

A mature person "who has needs" is someone who knows how to get them met effectively and intelligently. She knows when to ask for help and how to get it. An immature person "who is needy," gets bits and pieces of his or her life met, but tends to pay too high a price for them in the end. You can only land in a no-win trap if mere survival and avoiding sheer horror and pain is all you hope to accomplish.

Prepare now for the unexpected, while you have the energy and can take help without burning out your resources. It's important to remember that the little pig who took time to build the brick house got into less trouble than the one who settled for straw. The straw house doesn't take much labor from others. The brick house takes a crew and a foreman. Doing everything by yourself is living small, with little insight or vision for the future.

Often, those who are reluctant to ask for help have asked for help in the past and have been let down, and so they refuse to put themselves in that situation again. They go about life acting overly independent, saying they can do everything by themselves because they do it better, or because no one really understands or cares about their problems. These are only excuses. We use them when deep down we feel we don't really deserve any help.

It's adult to know what you need and to ask for it. It's childish to refuse help against your better judgment. This leads us to the next double-bind ingredient that may be bubbling in our stew.

NO-WIN TRAP INDUCER 5
Nothing in Reserve and Not Looking Ahead

When Noah built the ark, it wasn't raining.

It might seem funny to contemplate the above statement, but the reality is, we've all had a number of unexpected "floods" in our lives. You're bound to fall into a no-win trap if you're always living on the edge, leaving nothing in reserve. The more padding you have in your life, the less likely you'll end up in a double bind. Consider the following five points and see how well your stockpile stands up:

1. If you lost your job, alimony, or parents' inheritance tomorrow, would you be able to stay alive for at least three months?

2. If you locked yourself out of your house, do you know anyone you trust who would have the key?

3. If you're unavailable to pick up your child at school, is there someone else who could do it for you?

4. If your car breaks down, do you have another mode of transportation?

5. If your loved ones are out of town, do you have anyone with whom you could spend your holidays?

The point need not be belabored here, but it's important to take stock of the resources in your life. Certainly, money comes first to mind.

When meeting with a financial counselor one day about handling finances, I found myself surprised and embarrassed by a fairly obvious point he made. He said that it's important to pay yourself first, in the form of some sort of savings, before paying any bills to other people. That concept had never occurred to me.

To examine where I had been up to that point concerning finances and life in general, I didn't have to look far—I just had to open my checkbook. I'd always thought I was "responsible enough." But though I'd paid my bills on time, I unwittingly "robbed" myself, squandering what little savings I did accumulate and never putting anything away for my future. I made sure I had enough income to pay my bills to others, but I didn't create a healthy enough income flow for me. It never seemed that I could catch up with myself; it always felt like I was hanging on for dear life. (In truth, had I really seen life as so "dear," I wouldn't have treated myself so poorly.)

Then it dawned on me: The problem was much more than not having a budget plan or a well-tended stock portfolio. The problem was that *I had no plan at all.*

The only "plan" I had in life was that I would somehow make it to the next day, month, or year.

Having access to people who love and care about you, or who would at least help you out in a pinch, is becoming more necessary every day. While we may think, in this age of interconnectedness, that we're only a keystroke away from anything we could ever possibly need, there are days when your computer is down and your consultant has shut off his cell phone.

If you think you're doing fine without others, and you haven't gone out of your way to bring new resources and people into your life, wake up. You're heading for a no-win trap and a rude awakening.

NO-WIN TRAP INDUCER 6
Burning Bridges

Hopefully, by the time you've entered midlife, you'll be able to remember almost fondly a time when you were in a bad situation that left you clueless as to how you were going to get out. Such was the case with Margaret.

Margaret's Faulty Escape

The Chinese symbol for trouble is "Two women under one roof." That should have been stamped over the door of Margaret's in-laws' house.

Due to financial reasons, Margaret and her husband, John, found themselves living with his parents for a while, "until they got on their feet." One day, when Margaret felt she had no privacy, no money, and no way out, she chose to pick a fight with her husband and then proceeded to tell his mother everything she thought was wrong with her. She then picked up the keys to her car, packed what little she had, stormed out the front door, and yelled out to anyone who would listen, "I'm leaving and I'll never come back!"

Margaret got into her car, only to find that it wouldn't start. This was just as well, actually. She had nowhere else to go. But she'd just burned every bridge she had, and was left with nothing more than the tail between her legs. After what seemed like forever, she got out of the car, shuffled back inside, and somehow eventually got through the situation. Needless to say, however, the relationship was never the same again, and her marriage soon came to an end.

Years later she came to realize that in the heat of an angry moment, if you cut off your access to other people, the one you hurt the most is yourself. It brings up another Chinese proverb: "Being kind in an angry moment saves you 100 days of sorrow." Burning bridges is one of the bitterest ingredients of a no-win trap.

NO-WIN TRAP INDUCER 7
Being Hit with a Bomb

More than any other period in history, in the world today *anything* can happen. As globalization heats up the intensities and collisions of different factions at home and abroad, more and more people encounter life-changing situations in the everyday world. Whether you're being laid off from your job or are directly or indirectly affected by the threat of terrorism, sudden and unexpected disruptions in your life can compound whatever troubles are already plaguing you.

While any number of pressures and complications can be expected to arise during your lifetime, some crises—usually sudden and unanticipated—can be particularly overwhelming. The more you have your life sorted out and have dealt with the issues we've talked about, the more likely you are to survive these disasters. Before they happen, it's important to have your resources replenished, to have access to help, and to have your financial life in order. Which of the following "bombs" would you be especially vulnerable to?

- Having your significant other suddenly say, "I need time away from you to think."

- A child down the street goes missing and suddenly you're afraid for your own.

- Having a loved one die.

- A fire is raging through your neighborhood, and you realize you've locked yourself outside without your key.

- Finding out that "Dad" isn't your biological father.

- Realizing you have no water after a major earthquake hits.

- Your computer suddenly crashes.

- Discovering that your spouse is having an e-mail relationship.

- Being raped.

- Getting injured when you total your new car.

- Getting fired.

- Losing your home in a tornado or another type of disaster.

- Dropping your cell phone in your neighbor's pool.

Although some bombs are more devastating than others, they all disturb your mental stability and lower your resistance to physical illness. Extraordinary problems have a tendency to hit at a time when you're already overloaded with stress. They make it next to impossible for you to decide what to do next.

No two people respond to traumatic or stressful incidents in the same way. You may respond immediately. Or you may find yourself suppressing your feelings. If you do, they may resurface months or even years later, sometimes erupting in ways you'd never expect.

When you feel like a bomb has hit you, try not to make any hasty decisions. It's best to seek out someone to assist you, such as a counselor who can help you to see all the options that might be available to you. This is no time to pull up your bootstraps and go it alone. If you find yourself thinking, "I just don't want to be a burden," take these words out of your vocabulary. This is the time to call upon your safest and most understanding friend, family member, neighbor, spiritual or religious leader, or recommended professional. Seek help sooner rather than later.

The person who fails to recognize when he or she needs help can become a disaster waiting to happen. They're running on empty, and when they finally crash, they wreak havoc on those forced to take care of them. If you're concerned about being a burden, then make sure to get the help you need *before* you become a *real* burden, double-binding others with your overload of problems. Don't let your pride keep you from asking for help. There are times when your sense of embarrassment should be simply pushed aside.

You may find yourself feeling that your life will never be the same again. This may be true. When dramatic changes are occurring, acknowledge and then accept them, but at your own pace. It's no time to make rash decisions. Recognize that you may be in the beginning steps of a major transformation, where you'll not only come out different in the end, but better or wiser in some unpredictable way. Life isn't out to "get" you, even though it can seem that way. Don't force yourself to think you have to be overly strong to survive. Let people be there for you and help you through the difficult time. You deserve comfort and love. Sometimes it takes an act of devastation to let others in.

NO-WIN TRAP INDUCER 8
An Unrealistic Relationship with Time

Trying to get to your appointment across town in half the time it usually might take lands you with a traffic ticket or a major accident. While there are those who claim to be able to "shape shift" from one place to another in an instant of time, most of us have not progressed to that level. If you're one of those people with a bumper sticker that reads, "Always late but worth the wait," stop kidding yourself.

Having a realistic sense of time doesn't mean you're succumbing to someone else's need for authority. In actuality, it's quite the opposite. The more promptly you keep to the time you've promised, the more authority and respect you'll have from others, and the more you'll be able to enjoy your life.

Those who make the best use of their time are less inclined to fall into traps with themselves and uncomfortable places with others. Consider the following points to help improve your relationship with time. They could also help improve your relationship with others:

- If you realize you have a tendency to procrastinate on a project when left to your own devices, establish a routine whereby you recruit 1 to 3 people to serve as "project buddies." You then check in with them on a regular basis and let them know how you are doing. In having them help you be accountable for your own project, you are bound to get it done on time, or at least sooner than you would have by yourself. If you are inclined to get scattered, invite a buddy over to serve as an "overseer" or aid in helping you stay on task. We land ourselves in no-win traps when we insist we can do something by ourselves, but we never get it done. Just admit you need another person in on the deal, and don't prolong the agony by being such a "Lone Ranger."

- When you notice something is taking longer than you expected, check in with yourself to make sure you are giving the task the amount of attention it deserves, and not more than it deserves. If you have to make sure every last thing is exact to the point of being compulsive, you may want to consider that this way of life may not serve you well. Perfectionism is a no-win trap in and of itself, as it not only overspends precious time, but it adds anxiety as well. If you have this problem to the point of keeping you on the outs with life all too often, perhaps seeing a doctor who can assess your need for a medication can open a whole new possibility for less stress and less pitfalls along the way.

- Rather than landing in the doghouse with bosses and spouses, if you are running late, call and let them know rather than always having your tail between your legs. Believe it or not, the pain of being yelled at over the phone is actually less harsh than being chastised for not calling at all.

NO-WIN TRAP INDUCER 9
Equations That Just Don't Work

While none of us would think of insisting that $3 + 2 = 7$, many of us live our lives on similarly illogical premises. How we think is how we speak, and how we speak is how we live. Our thoughts and statements about ourselves and others are actually the links on the chain that lead from one place to another. If you find yourself wondering, "How did I ever get myself into this?" look back and consider the "equations" you've been *living into* your life. Here are a few examples from my own life and the lives of others:

"If my marriage doesn't work out, I'll just get divorced."

"I'll take it just this once. They'll never know."

"Why shouldn't I get myself another piece of jewelry? He spends money we don't have at the track."

"I know I should leave him, but he promised he wouldn't hit me again. Besides, all men have something wrong with them."

"I know I hate my job, but the money's so good."

"I can't go back to college. I'll lose my health benefits."

"Things never work out for me."

"Other people have all the luck."

"I never have time to finish anything."

"I always get stuck holding the bag."

"Anything I do isn't good enough."

While you may believe your casual comments will never amount to much, it is important to recognize that for every comment you hear yourself mutter, you've probably sent that same message to your unconscious many times more. Whether stated one time or a million, there is truth to the notion that every thought and expression inevitably goes somewhere. It is interesting and at times sad to note that if you believe no one ever hears or sees you, the unconscious inside you does hear and does take you seriously.

If you don't want your future to be like your past, don't speak of it like you expect it will happen to you again tomorrow.

Before going on to the next chapter, make a point of writing down five statements that are actually equations you *want* to live into. Consider the following examples.

"I know I'll get the help I need to get this job done."

"Every day I'm getting closer to my goals."

"I sure am glad it's easy to say 'I'm sorry' when I'm wrong."

"It's truly amazing how the right people always seem to come along."

It's one thing to get caught up in blindly mimicking Pollyanna-like statements to yourself and others while having no sincere intention of following through. It's quite another to commit to what truly resonates with you as being something worth your solid focus and intention. In the book *You Can Heal Your Life*, Louise Hay says that different physical ailments can be symptomatic of particular inner, and at times outer, negative conversations. You may or may not notice you're thinking this way, but you are breathing in your beliefs right along with the air you take into your lungs.

We actually live and breathe right into our beliefs until they become concrete and real. That is why, if you don't like what you're thinking, then you won't like how you'll be living. It's why you need to be as conscious and disciplined about your thoughts, words, and actions as possible. Life presents us with enough challenges. Don't cloud your potential for happiness with your own double-binded thinking. Give your Self and your future a chance. In case you need a jump start in the right direction, try these phrases out for size:

> "Even though I see no solution for my issue right now, I'm willing to be open to finding one."

> "Even though I'm not very satisfied with how my life is going right now, I'm determined and appreciate and acknowledge everything that is going well."

> "One thing I know: There will be a day when I look back at this and know I got through all right to the other side."

Give yourself credit. There are times in life when we just have to start with an equation we can live with and work up from. The important part is keeping a grip on which way is up, and not adding trouble to an already complex situation.

I once worked with a wonderful teenage boy who had gotten into trouble at school and simply stated, "I try to do the right thing with the wrong people." When he realized how hilarious that statement really was, we both began to laugh. I then told him I was also laughing at myself. Isn't it amazing how often we try to do the "right" thing with the "wrong" people?

We'll finish this chapter with a recap of the nine no-win trap inducers. Ponder the notion that if people had nine lives the way cats apparently do, every time you engage in one of these no-win trap inducers, you're knocking off the possibility of one of your lives. The less you fall into any one of these patterns, the more you'll be able to land on your feet.

QUICK GUIDE TO THE NO-WIN TRAP INDUCERS

1. *Expecting More Than People Can Give.* Recognize when someone just can't give you what you want. It's generally not because they're withholding love from you and you're to blame. It's just that they aren't able to give it the way you want.

2. *Not Recognizing Entropy.* Be careful not to put your energy and effort where it won't be well-received.

3. *Not Taking Care of Yourself.* Grow up. There's no freedom like being accountable.

4. *Not Getting Help When You Need It.* You'll never be a burden when you can ask for help while you can still make use of it.

5. *Nothing in Reserve and Not Looking Ahead.* Planning and saving for a rainy day keeps you freed up to enjoy your life and ensure a roof over you head. You'll also have more choices and options.

6. *Burning Bridges.* Life is long when you don't have access to what you need. Make a point to leave the door open when parting ways. You don't have to go away angry, you can just go away. Every experience leads to the next one. You never know when you'll need help from an old contact again.

7. *Being Hit with a Bomb.* This is not a time in history to pretend life circumstances can't change quickly. The more you're prepared, the less foxholes you'll have to dig.

8. *An Unrealistic Relationship with Time.* Start to live your life as if you always have 15 minutes to spare. Don't add to life's predicaments by crowding too much into one day. That's just looking for speed traps and trouble.

9. *Equations That Just Don't Work.* Check in with yourself each day, and tell yourself what your game plan is. If it doesn't add up or you're pushing your luck, change your line of thinking to realistically work for you.

In the next chapter, you'll read about various ways people respond to no-win traps. The more you recognize the way you tend to respond, the better your chances will be of changing the responses that don't work for you. The more you see where you are, the better the chance you have of finding a way out and moving on. Perhaps you'll see, too, that like the teenage boy I spoke about, sometimes you've just been trying to do the right thing with the wrong people. Once you get a better feel for what's been going on, you'll be better able to see double binds coming and step out of the way.

3

Common Responses to No-Win Traps

I don't know the key to success, but the key to failure is trying to please everyone.

Bill Cosby

*W*hile it might appear that we don't create the no-win trap, that other people double-bind us and lure us into impossible circumstances, *we* are actually the ones who entrap ourselves. *We* are the ones who allow ourselves to be overly influenced by other people's opinions and attitudes, and by our own desire to please others before pleasing ourselves. It is the *meaning* we give to the situation that determines how deeply we fall into the trap. In fact, the meaning we give it is the only reason the "trap" exists at all. We are the creators of our own story.

There are times when you're truly fighting for your life, and times when you only make it seem that way. It's important to know the difference between the two. In those moments when you feel you're up against the wall, when it seems the only thing you can do is stand there and take it, you may find yourself hoping that something or someone will magically come to carry you away and end your impossible dilemma. The reality is, while it is not exactly magic, there is someone available to come to your rescue: That person is you.

You may not physically remove yourself from your present situation, at least not right away, but starting now—even this minute—you have a choice in deciding how *emotionally invested* you're willing to be. That includes how upset you'll allow yourself to be, what responsibility you're willing to take, even how much or how little you believe you need to explain yourself to others.

In the end, you're the one who determines how you respond to others and to outside influences. You're the one who decides how much importance to attach to a person or situation. Once you begin to recognize that it's not in your best interest to try to change or influence other people, but to simply evolve into your own person, you'll find that you have far more freedom. Others will begin to realize they can't manipulate you, and will be less inclined to "keep you in their clutches." In essence, you'll stop giving your power away.

How do you go about doing this? How do you become the balanced person who can discern the difference between the people and circumstances that are healthy for you and those that are only pulling you down?

One place to start is to examine the ways you currently relate to people and situations—on first meeting them, and how your interactions go over time. As you read about the various responses to double binds presented in this chapter, notice which ones you relate to the most. Becoming aware of unhealthy patterns of thought and behavior is the first best step you can take toward change.

OCCASIONAL VERSUS INTRACTABLE DOUBLE BINDS

Learning to accept people as they are is one of life's most difficult tasks. If a no-win entanglement occurs only occasionally with someone and involves one particular theme that mainly affects that individual—such as gaining a few pounds or nervousness before hosting a party—it's probably not worth driving yourself crazy about. As long as other areas of the relationship are fine and you truly value this person, a few verbal confrontations shouldn't bother you too much. You may just have to accept these occasional volleys, knowing that they'll eventually blow over. Of course, the time may come when you'll want to discuss your feelings in order to clear the air. But if handled sensitively, this can have a beneficial effect. The other person may even thank you for bringing it to his or her attention.

In more difficult, intractable double binds, however, annoying issues appear more often and refuse to just blow over. It's also likely, if you try to talk about them, the response you get will be anything but grateful.

The trick in all this, then, is to be able to discern between double binds that are serious, insolvable problems and those that are merely occasional annoyances. Understanding the nature of the double bind you're in is the first step to avoiding them and finding your way out.

The following is a commonplace double-bind scenario. It shows how double binds often get started and how easy it is to fall into a trap.

BETWEEN A ROCK AND A HARD PLACE

Your girlfriend, with whom life usually goes well, asks you how she looks in her new dress. You're honest. "You look great," you tell her. "Beautiful."

"You're just saying that," she replies, "because you think it's what I want you to say."

You had no intention of patronizing her. "No, really, you do look good."

"Good—not great. What you really mean is I look fat."

You roll your eyes. "This is crazy!"

"I knew it," she replies. "You hate this dress."

You had no idea that your truthful compliment could bring your girlfriend to an identity crisis, but her next statement reveals just how worthless she really feels.

"You always make me feel rotten about myself. You're always putting me down."

Of course, you haven't put her down. You've only responded positively to a loaded question.

Unfortunately, there was no right answer. You were lured into a double bind. Chances are, no one could have handled the situation any better. Any approach would have ended up wrong.

If you get stuck in feeling you're guilty, at fault, or inept because you couldn't make this woman feel good about herself (certainly the sexes can be switched here), then your low self-esteem is actually colluding with hers. If, however, you quickly grasp that this is just an issue she has going on with herself, that she's only trying to pull you into it, you can step aside and simply wait for it to blow over. If it doesn't, just refuse to be roped in.

Consider the way this young husband brilliantly handled his wife's bad day.

Gwendolyn and the Beautiful Omelet

Gwendolyn and George had recently gotten married. They were adorable together, and had just moved into a brand-new town house. While George was at the office, working eight hours and more a day at his new computer-programming job, Gwen was home studying for her RN exam, which was quickly approaching. She'd been studying day and night, with hardly any sleep for the past two weeks, when George came home and found her storming around the house in an unusually bad mood.

This was not her general tenor. In the two and a half years they'd been together, George had never seen her so upset. He knew her test was that Saturday, and that the pressure was making her uptight. So he said, "Honey, you look like you're having a bad day. I'm starving and would like to make dinner. Can I make you an omelet?"

Gwen stopped her mindless puttering and muttering for a second. "Yeah, I guess I'll have an omelet. I've been so upset over this stupid test, I've forgotten to eat all day."

George went into the kitchen and prepared dinner. When Gwen came in, she sat down in a lump and seemed to stare at the wall. George presented her with a perfectly wonderful plate of fluffy eggs with cheese and onions, just the way she liked them. She looked at it and started to cry. She began to complain that he had it so easy, he had no test to take and only had to work every day. She said he had no idea what it was like for her, studying all by herself, day in and day out, with no one to talk to.

George knew there was no way he could win. He knew that if he spoke up now, it would just provoke her more, and if he said nothing, she'd say he had no ability to empathize. So he just sat there, settling in for a long evening. Somewhere in his mind, he was able to grasp the fact that this dilemma was *time-limited*. Once the exam was over, the odds were high that he'd have his true love back. Gwendolyn jabbed her fork into her omelet over and over, finally dropping it onto the plate. She ran crying from the table and into their bedroom. Still George just sat there, saying nothing, recognizing there was no use interjecting. Gwendolyn slammed the door and yelled out, "I'm too tired to eat. I'm going to bed."

George ate his omelet, watched some television, and got into bed about 10:30 p.m. Gwendolyn was tossing and turning, obviously exhausted. George lay down beside her, gently stroked her hair and kissed the top of her head. She turned around and hugged him tightly, cried, and told him she was sorry about ruining their dinner. Gradually, she became more coherent, and told him she'd never been so tired or so beside herself.

Looking at her lovingly George held her in his arms. He told her he knew she was overwhelmed, and he offered to bring her something to eat in bed. Gwen looked up like a little girl and asked if her eggs were still available. George smiled and said, "As a matter of fact, they are. They're more liked scrambled eggs now, but they're still edible." He got up, heated them in the microwave, and brought them back into the room.

Gwen ate as if she hadn't had a bite for weeks. When she was through, she put the plate down and thanked George for being so nice about everything. She looked apologetically into his eyes and asked, "How come you didn't get mad at me when I jabbed my fork in the eggs?"

George looked at her and smiled. "Why honey," he said, "that's not my job."

Double-bind "invitations" like these can be seen as a kind of test. If you accept the invitation, you're guaranteed trouble. But if you stand back and see it as an internal conflict the person is having, you can simply be loving and let it go by. Standing back and yet being available, not getting angry or holding a grudge (even if the person verbally taunts you) is the surest way to keep an occasional double bind just that—occasional.

HANGING AROUND FOR THE CARROT

Perhaps your no-win situation begins to escalate. You find as time goes on that you say or do the right thing less and less, according to the other person. There are times when you get so upset you could scream.

But the relationship is not completely intolerable. Indeed, in certain areas it seems to be flourishing. So you tell yourself to focus on the good things and try to ignore the bad. You hope for more victories. You imagine how wonderful things could be. You grow increasingly determined to stay "in the game." You continue to tell yourself this works for you—"at least for now."

You're like the donkey that keeps moseying along, reaching for the carrot on the stick. But the carrot is always just out of reach, and you never seem to be getting anywhere.

You survive on a diet of illusions. When the other person is pleased, you feel momentarily accepted. You think you were able to make them happy. And when they become mad or discontent with someone else and complain about them endlessly, you find yourself gleefully listening—mainly because you're glad it isn't you. However, because you know that at any moment you could join their ranks, you feel like you're walking on eggshells all the time.

If double-bind dilemmas with a few "wins" thrown in seem familiar and even acceptable to you, take a look at what this is telling you about yourself. What exactly is the price you're paying for the "good" stuff? Do you feel you deserve better? And if you do, can this situation or person actually provide it for you? Do you stop to ask yourself these questions, or is this just how life seems to be?

These double-bind scenarios are like an old pair of worn-out shoes. You tell yourself they're actually quite comfortable, even though they don't reflect the person you'd really like to be. You've had this pair for years, however; they've traveled with you many places. But just how long can you put up with those holes? Is this what little you think you deserve? Do you really believe you can wear them into happiness?

It's amazing how much pain we're willing to tolerate, especially if we get some small reward now and then. Sometimes it's better to walk barefoot for a while, until you find the pair of shoes that's truly meant for you. That is, if you can stand the sometimes long and lonely road ahead.

This next case has a mixture of interpersonal and situational double binds. Watch what happens when a circuit overload comes into play.

Wes's Promotion

Wes loved his job. In fact, his work was all he knew. He had joined a prestigious law firm of tax attorneys right out of law school, after graduating tenth in his class at the age of 28. The most senior partner, and Wes's boss, known in the firm as "the grande old man," treated Wes as if he were his own son. Wes had never been his father's favorite, so this was especially enticing to him.

At first it seemed Wes could do no wrong. He was entrusted with some of the best cases. Wes went out to lunch and dinner with his most important clients and the senior partners. Wes even pinch-hit for his boss on major cases when he was out of town. Wes worked 12-to-14-hour days, taking work home every weekend and rarely going on vacation. He did whatever was asked of him, and he was grateful when his boss invited him to his home on Thanksgiving and Christmas.

Over time, as Wes's boss became more comfortable with him, he began to admonish Wes in front of the other attorneys and clients in the office. He'd blame Wes for losing documents he himself had misplaced, or for losing cases that were in fact lost due to his own blunders. Yet when they were alone, Wes's boss would tell him that he cared for Wes as if he were his own son, and that he would surely be a partner soon. Through it all, Wes always hung in there, taking the brunt and waiting for the inevitable promotion.

Three years passed. When Wes finally sat down for his annual review, he fully expected he would be promoted to partner. It didn't happen. His boss explained that the other young attorneys who had been there longer than Wes (and actually brought in more money to the firm by bringing their own book of clients) had been complaining to the other partners that they hadn't been promoted yet. He added that this put him in an uncomfortable position, so he decided to promote one of the other lawyers in the firm.

At first, Wes was devastated. But after going out to dinner with his boss, and realizing he was still the senior partner's favorite, he settled back into his 14-hour-a-day groove. Besides, his boss promised that the next promotion to partner would be his.

Two more years went by. Tired of working so hard and having almost nothing to show for it but a house that was empty most of the time, Wes decided to leave early one night and attend an alumni function at his alma mater. While there, he met a brilliant woman, Liz, who had just graduated the year before and was now working near his office.

They began dating. Soon, Wes was seeing Liz so often he could barely keep up with his work for the law firm. His priorities gradually began to change, and for the first time in his life he could honestly say he was happy. But now that he had more in his life than he really wanted, his circuits began to overload.

Wes knew he'd have to find some sort of a balance, but he didn't know how to get off the hamster wheel of work. One night, staying even later than usual at the office to clean up an important case, he looked out the window. He noticed Liz, his budding romance, walking out of a nightclub down the street, arm in arm with two male colleagues. He was appalled, but tried not to jump to conclusions. He remembered he'd been invited out with this same group the week before, but had turned the invitation down because he'd had so much work to do.

At that moment, Wes made a decision. He would no longer live his life like a workhorse with no reward. He closed up the office and went home.

The next day, he got up and sent flowers to Liz. Then he called her and asked her out for dinner, not mentioning what he'd seen the night before. Liz happily said yes. Wes then strode into the office and asked to see the senior partner, his boss. With a firm strength and maturity he'd never demonstrated before, he asked him when his promotion to partnership would actually occur.

His boss was taken aback, and Wes pressed on, neither raising his voice nor cowering at the thought that his boss might be displeased. Rather than focusing on thoughts of rejection, Wes simply sat and waited, thinking about the other places he might have to look for work. Wes had finally realized that if this plan didn't pan out, he had other options.

After a few long minutes, the senior partner turned to Wes and, speaking directly to him, said he was doing a great job, that he knew Wes had gotten him out of more messes than he cared to remember. What's more, his own clients were calling Wes more often than they called him, and he realized he needed Wes even more than Wes needed him. He told Wes then that he was glad he'd brought up the matter of his promotion and that he'd get back to him by the end of the week.

The following day, Wes got a memo that his promotion would be announced at the next partners' meeting. It came along with an invitation to a "partners only" dinner that Friday night.

Wes sat back and smiled to himself. Thanks to his circuit overload and a determination to get what he truly wanted in life, he had finally stood up for himself and demanded to be heard. It had worked. He vowed he would continue to work hard, but that he would use his time more wisely, making sure to fit Liz into his schedule.

Does this story seem too good to be true? For those who feel it's their lot in life to clean up after everyone else and be the last one out of the office, it may be. But to those who are willing to reevaluate their lives, clearly it's not. That's the purpose of discomfort in any situation. It gives you the opportunity to check in on yourself, to realize what you're worth, and to take the risks necessary to get what you deserve. Wes's life actually turned for the better when he dared to go after the things he really wanted.

Are you always hanging around for the carrot? It's not easy to know how realistic it is to wait for a desired reward. Here are a few questions you may want to ask yourself:

- Think about your major relationships and circumstances: work, school, club, commute, marriage, finances, family, friends. Is there a relationship or situation that started out well but is now impossible more than 40 percent of the time?

- Are you hanging on to it because you think you get some type of benefit you couldn't get elsewhere?

- Does this person, situation, or service do something that you believe you can't do for yourself?

- Does the situation go back and forth between the sublime and the awful?

- Do you accept that anguish and suffering will always be part of your relationship with this person or situation?

- Do you feel this situation is your only option, so you have to put all your energy into it?

- Do you take the attitude that others have it a lot worse, so you're actually lucky to be in your barely tolerable situation?

- Do you feel you're putting more energy into the relationship than the other person, and it still isn't enough?

- Do you feel others can "have it all," but you can only have part of your life the way you want it?

- What if another job became available? What if you met people who treated you better? If you had options that offered better results and less frustration, would your current situation seem more intolerable to you?

If you answered yes to any of these questions, you may be hanging around for the carrot—a carrot with a higher price than you can afford.

THE FIX-IT SYNDROME

You wish you could turn back the clock and have another chance to do things over again. You have a burning need to either be right or to come up with the correct response. You bang your head against the wall at times, insisting that if you could only find the right formula, you'd actually have a chance at winning the game.

You're caught in the Fix-It Syndrome.

Unfortunately, there is no way to "win" in a double bind. The situation is doomed from the start. Double binds keep you—as well as everyone else—in a state of constant chaos. They are self-designed mazes without any exit. Wandering around in that maze, your unconscious keeps telling you, "If only I can be more perfect, everything will turn out fine." That's about as useful as saying, "Perhaps if I hit my head with a hammer enough, it will actually stop hurting."

When you're singing this tune, you're determined to believe that fighting a losing battle is better than cutting your losses and going home. It's almost always a mistake, especially when you're busy running around, trying to force an intolerable situation to work, and don't take the time to stop and carefully evaluate what's really actually taking place.

The fact is, you probably believe you need to be connected to this drama for some reason you may not even realize, and the only way of connecting to it is the one you know. Even though disconnecting physically or detaching emotionally could create a better life for you in the long run, the thought of being alone or making major changes seems too frightening to handle at this time.

The good news here is that you don't necessarily have to leave the relationship or situation altogether, at least not right away. You can begin to create new ways of connecting to the place or person you're with, and from there you can create new options and determine which way you want to go.

Take a look at the following case, and notice how the desire to "fix it" ends up creating a no-win trap.

John, the Husband Who Never Went Out

Ann was an outdoor person. John was an indoor person. When they got married, Ann became determined to turn John into a tennis player. (After all, he'd hit some balls with her while they were dating, which was more than her own dad ever did.) At first John would squawk about going to play tennis, but at least he made an effort and did it. He actually seemed to have a good time when they played, and on one occasion he even voiced a desire to enter a mixed doubles tournament. Ann took this as a sign that he was an athlete in the making, and she bought him a racket for his birthday. (Any sign of life out of John always sent her into a frenzy of enthusiasm.)

After much coaxing on Ann's part and complaining on his, John finally did join her in the tournament. To Ann's delight, they came in third place. From that day on, Ann made it her business that she and John would become "the" tennis couple of the local tennis club, which, at Ann's insistence, they finally joined.

Years went by and John and Ann had three children. Needless to say, all three children played tennis, which John encouraged because that kept Ann preoccupied and she therefore focused less on him. He had given up playing tennis altogether. While Ann had hoped he'd show more enthusiasm for this potential family activity, she was glad that at least he took the kids to their lessons (though he never stayed to watch them play).

Ann had put herself into a strange double bind. The more she pushed her husband to go out and spend time on the court with her and the kids, the more he'd pout, lock himself into the basement with a beer, and piddle around with his tools for hours on end. If she never said anything, he'd just keep to himself.

In time, Ann and the children got more engrossed in activities and sports of all kinds, while John became even more lethargic and lazy. Ann gave up on trying to get him to do anything at all with the family. She even started making up excuses for why he never did anything with her and the kids. If she couldn't "fix" the problem by getting John involved, she'd at least try and cover it up by explaining the problem away. Everytime one of the children complained to her that Dad never did anything, or they went to ask Dad directly to go somewhere, Ann quickly took them aside and told them how Dad worked very hard and needed to rest—although she was steaming inside to see how rejected her kids felt and how much of a couch potato her husband had become.

Ann had just about given up on trying to get John to change his ways when one day she announced to him that they hadn't been out of the house together as a couple or as a family for over two years. John looked over at her and said nothing. Then he turned away and flicked the remote control to another channel.

Ann was completely discouraged. She became dizzy, thinking that this was how it would be for the rest of her life. A few days later, for no reason in particular, she went to check a drawer in John's side of the room, where she'd seen him go several times when he thought no one was looking. She opened it, afraid to see what was inside, and found a prescription bottle of very strong pain pills that was almost empty. John had gotten them years ago for a successful reconstructive knee surgery he'd had. The prescription, Ann noticed, had been refilled many times since.

There it was: a big part of the reason John was so inactive and kept to himself. It had never occurred to Ann that John had been severely depressed and overwhelmed by life, and was using the television and the refuge of the basement to shield himself from any more expectations than he already had at work. She'd been completely unaware that he had a hidden addiction to pain pills. She'd always thought that the beer he drank every day was just something to help him relax.

That night, when the kids had gone to bed, she went down to the basement to bring John a glass of milk and some cookies she'd made that day. She hadn't been this considerate to him when they'd been alone in months, and John instinctively knew something must be up. He barely looked up at her, took the glass of milk and the plate of cookies, and thanked her while he continued watching reruns on TV.

Ann sat down next to him and quietly told him she'd found the pills. John launched into a tirade about how terrible she was for going through his personal stuff, but Ann just sat quietly and didn't respond. After John sat back down, amazed at Ann's calm reaction, she said, "John, I'm not here to condemn you or tell you off about all this. I'm only saying that I found these pills and I think you're hurting and need a lot of help. I also feel uncomfortable about the way you always seem to have a beer in your hand. If you want to talk about it or go to a doctor for help, I'm behind you. I will not approach you about this again."

She left the basement then, and John sat in stunned silence. He couldn't believe how she'd cut directly to the crux of his issue. Meanwhile, she slumped down on a couch upstairs in the living room, exhausted from the extreme self-control of her performance. She'd always vowed to never yell at her husband the way her own mother did whenever she'd caught her father drinking. Ann promised herself she'd go to Alanon, and that she wouldn't lose any more power by repeating herself and acting like a nag.

After that night, things began to change in John and Ann's household. Ann no longer tried to stand in the way of the kids approaching John about anything, and she focused more on her own life. She got into therapy, went to Codependents Anonymous self-help sessions, and began taking her work and career as a legal secretary more seriously, realizing there might come a day when she'd have to lean more heavily on her own income than she did now. She also realized how thankful she was that John did work and make a good living, and she began to tell him so more often.

Seeing all this, John became more active with the kids and told Ann he was thinking about going into drug rehab for alcohol and pain pills. He even began watching TV with them upstairs in the living room. Ann had learned from her therapist and the weekly meetings that she should stay out of the "fix-it" person role, so she simply, supportively, told her husband that she thought his idea was a good one, and left it at that.

Somewhere along the line, some old tape in Ann had snapped. She saw that she'd been running on empty for far too long, trying to make everything look better than it was, and she finally just refused to do that anymore. It's hard to tell which way this marriage will go in the long run, but one thing is for sure: Ann will never again be the fix-it person. She'd finally come to see the major role she played in creating her own double bind.

What would you have done if you were Ann? What would you do if you were John? The way Ann ultimately handled the situation in this case was exemplary. But it required her to change from being the person she'd been. If you've been in a no-win trap as long as Ann has, it's important to recognize that *the only way to change your outer circumstance is to alter your own approach.* Only then can the situation improve.

While it would have been understandable for Ann to be upset, yelling and carrying on at John would only have served as a convenient distraction, allowing John to focus on how "mean and angry" his wife was, rather than on how his own addiction was ruining his life and the life of his family. Chances are he would have blamed her for his problems.

When you're dubbed a fix-it person in terms of double binds, the only kind of fixing that's going on is keeping the never-ending no-win game in place. You may well be right about what's wrong with your situation, but it won't get any better if you're not willing to change yourself.

Are You a Fix-It Person?

Here are some questions to ask yourself to determine if you're trying to fix something in vain:

- Have you tried everything, but nothing has worked? Do you continue to try even harder?

- Have you offered the others involved a workable plan that would be helpful to everyone, but no one is interested? Or do you avoid talking about the issues that bother you altogether?

- Do you find yourself saying, "This situation would be fine if only the other person would change?" yet you're aware that they won't change, at least not in the present arrangement.

- Have you genuinely tried to see things from a different perspective, and when you do, there's still no resolution?

- Does everything seem to get worse the more you try?

- Have you learned something from this dilemma, but you feel the other party never has?

- Have you considered the idea of "fixing" this scenario by focusing on what to change about yourself? Have you made some minor, and even major, changes to no avail?

If your answer to most of these questions is yes, you may want to consider stepping outside the picture emotionally and withdrawing your energy from the situation. That way, you can run your own life without being entangled in the drama. Those who choose to stay emotionally tied to double-bind relationships and situations would do well to consider the following points:

- Realize that, given the way you're currently responding, the other party is unlikely to change.

- If you can't accept the person or situation as is, without judgment, put your effort into altering your approach, not theirs.

- Stop trying to force others into your game plan. Also, consider the possibility that your behavior has been more of the problem than the solution, however much you feel you are "right."

- If it's a work situation, start looking for another job without announcing it to your coworkers.

If taking any of these steps seems impossible for you to accept or do, you'd probably do well to remove yourself physically, or detach emotionally from the situation, at least for a while. Sometimes a vacation or a break, without making a big deal about it, can be good for you and everyone involved.

BEING THE SCAPEGOAT

Often when you feel that others are impossible to deal with, you find yourself the target for everyone else's blame. Consider the story of the Greek messenger.

As the narrative goes, in the olden days of Greece, a messenger would run from town to town to report news and cultural events of the day. When he reported on wars, murders, or deaths, it was so upsetting to those who heard the news that they sometimes killed the messenger. It was as if killing the bringer of bad news would take away the problem itself.

"Fools go where angels dare not tread." Without realizing it, well-meaning individuals often go daringly out on a limb to please others or to give them feedback about themselves that may be taken the wrong way. For example, when asked to give an opinion to someone at a family gathering or a business meeting, a scapegoat might mistakenly see it as a chance to share what they and everyone else are really thinking. However, to their surprise, rather than enlightening the throng around them, they've only dug themselves a hole. While they may have an IQ that's higher than the others, or at least are attempting to help, they're not demonstrating a whole lot of "emotional intelligence."

Scapegoats are often very bright individuals who are creative in many ways, with many talents that go undeveloped. All too often they spend most of their energy either trying to get others out of some impossible entanglement or are up to their ears in alligators themselves, due to misplaced efforts of their own. They impulsively jump in before anyone else, without considering the lay of the land.

The scapegoat serves as a tension release for those around him. Quite often, the person who is relegated to the scapegoat position is so sensitive to the tension in the air that he would actually rather bare the brunt of everyone else's wrath than keep quiet and pretend the problem isn't there. He's probably not consciously aware of why he responds the way he does, he just knows he wants to help.

For example, two brothers who head up a business may constantly fight. They hire an innocent third party, an employee, who answers to both of them. This person receives contradictory orders, gets caught in the middle, and consequently is blamed for things that go wrong.

The success of a double-bind operation like this depends on the sacrificial lamb. If the third party tries to sidestep the situation, he may succeed if he knows how to detach himself and thus avoid being blamed. This requires discipline and self-control, deliberately staying out of the ring when the brothers begin to disagree. When asked for his opinion, he must be careful. Pleasing one brother is likely to offend the other, bringing blame on himself. It's important for this person to just do his job and lay low. In fact, if he's really smart about it, he'll be looking for a job while he fulfills his most basic duties. He'll leave as soon as possible, after learning everything he can about how to stay out of the middle.

Scapegoats are bred and developed in families. Unfortunately, part of the "development" in becoming a scapegoat generally includes feeling devalued and even ostracized much of the time. If you played this role in your family and didn't make an effort to stop it, or didn't realize it was going on, chances are you're still playing it out in your life.

Consider the following true case. How far are you willing to go to win approval from those who are close to you?

Ben, the Son Who Didn't Donate a Kidney

Ben's bladder never did work very well, an incapacity he'd apparently inherited from his father. In fact, ever since he was a young boy, he had trouble in school due to his need to frequently urinate. This caused him a lot of embarrassment, and he was often harassed by other schoolchildren. Ben got used to it, however. After all, he'd had plenty of practice at home, where he was taunted by whoever was in a bad mood that day.

It seemed as if Ben was the stepchild and his two sisters, Mary Anne and Beth, could do no wrong. When Ben got As and Bs in school, while his sisters could barely get by with Cs, his parents expected him to maintain his high grades, even as the girls received special privileges and gifts whenever they merely managed to bring home a B.

Ben couldn't understand it. The harder he tried to please and do well, the more he was written off by his family. It seemed to him that his sisters were praised if they could walk across the street and chew gum at the same time.

In time, Ben became sadly accustomed to the skewed display of attention in his family. In fact, there were times he almost prided himself on being able to take what was being dished out to him. He'd dismiss it with clever comebacks that sometimes made the family laugh but more often made them angry with him for days, especially when he showed up his sisters by pointing out how much more intelligent he was, and how much better in art.

The truth was, Ben intimidated his family. This included his parents, who were insecure about never having accomplished the things they set out to do in life. In later years, Ben's mother told him he would never come and sit on her lap like his sisters did, or let her hold him for very long. As a little boy, Ben had preferred the company of his uncle, who playfully roughhoused with him more than his sickly father ever would. Sometimes his father was even jealous.

Ben didn't realize all this, and didn't find out about it until years later, when his father needed a kidney transplant and asked him for help. While Ben thought he was the least favorite child in the family, everyone came running to him when there was a family crisis. Whenever he saved the day, it was taken for granted. And if he was unable to pull a family member out of some mess they'd created, he was an outcast for days afterward.

So when his father approached Ben, who was a 29-year-old adult now, to consider donating one of his kidneys, it came as no surprise to Ben. Of course his father would never have asked his sisters, even though they had less trouble with their bladder or kidneys than he did. That had always been the way it went.

Ben said no. He was deeply involved in law school and in no position to take time out for an extensive operation. On top of that, his own health was fragile. So for the first time in his life, he refused one of his father's major requests.

His entire family acted appalled. They didn't call him for months. He wasn't even invited home for Thanksgiving.

Ben was not surprised by their behavior. And in fact he was relieved, and even pleased by his own response to his father's request. For the first time in his life, he had stood up and taken care of himself. He knew that no one else would, and he refused to jeopardize his schooling, his career, and his health. He had finally come to the conclusion that his family would never be kind and loving to him no matter what he did.

When he was ostracized, Ben gave up trying to get anyone from the family to call him. It was a few months into the next year when one of his sisters called to say that she had donated a kidney to Dad, and everyone was doing okay. Since then, Ben has had contact with his family, seeing them from time to time, but they make no more major requests that could put him in jeopardy. They're not particularly close, but now Ben senses more respect from them for who he is.

Are You Playing the Role of the Scapegoat?

Does this case seem at all familiar to you? Do you think you'd be the person who would have donated the kidney no matter how much it interfered with or hurt your life? Or would you have been able to focus on your needs and taken care of yourself?

It's important for each one of us to look within and determine what motivates us to be there for other people when it's damaging to us. It's also important to examine whether the way you engage in relationships is working for you. If you think it might be possible that you're playing the scapegoat role, consider the following questions:

1. Were there often times as a child when, unable to tolerate a given situation, you pointed it out to family members to no avail? Are there often times now when you do the same to coworkers, and the comments are ill-received?

2. Have you willingly or unwillingly become a spokesperson for a group that encourages you to speak out for them? Yet, when you do this, do they all stand back and act shocked, as if they don't know what you're even talking about?

3. Have you been the brunt of others' jokes and had the thought, "This must be the way life will always be for me?" Perhaps you never questioned the role, and in fact told yourself you liked the attention.

4. As a child or adult, were you ever the scapegoat for someone's anger? They were actually angry with someone else, but took it out on you because you were available. Perhaps you felt you were required to take it.

5. As a child, if something was spilled, broken, or missing, did you often get the blame even when you didn't do it? If you made a mistake or didn't express yourself the way others thought you should, were you berated about it to the point where you finally lashed out or shut down?

6. Have you ever been forced to take sides or referee family members when they were feuding? Were you then left on the outside, or possibly considered the instigator who started the fighting in the first place?

7. Are there times when you feel your idea is the best way to go in a group situation, and although no one wants to hear it, you insist on voicing your opinion anyway?

Just one yes answer could mean you have been, and possibly still are, a scapegoat—a willing victim who stands in a negative spotlight. The more yes answers you gave, the more programmed you probably are to being a scapegoat.

A good exercise to do over the next few days is to watch the dynamics of people in your household, at work, and in the world at large. Observe who seems to get blamed for things and who appears to get away with everything. Where do you fit into this picture? How does this affect your life? Remember, you don't have to be the sacrificial lamb in order to get love and appreciation—even if it's been your pattern in the past. It's important to make sure you have love for yourself, and that you don't allow yourself to be used and abused.

BEING THE MARTYR

In the world of no-win traps, the scapegoat is actually more positive about his circumstance in life than the martyr. The scapegoat has hopes—whether real or imagined—that at some point he'll be appreciated or even seen as a hero. The martyr, on the other hand, makes a career of disappointment. She knows for sure she'll never be appreciated or acknowledged in the way she wants and deserves to be. In fact, that's her claim to fame, and the only kind of joy she ever has.

Being the martyr doesn't necessarily mean you see yourself as the rejected one in your family or at work. You probably feel you're the only one who knows how to do anything right or make everyone feel okay. You're sure that if it weren't for you, no one else would be able to make it.

Part of your story is that everyone uses you. You assume they want something from you—to make money, to cook dinner, to pay the bills—and that that's all you're good for. Of course, you get no pleasure out of it, but somehow you're always available whenever someone needs you.

It could be that your "need to be needed" is so strong that you're willing to sacrifice your life for others. It could also be that a part of you, deep down, fears that if the person you're with could take care of him- or herself, they'd leave you. This goes for spouses, lovers, children, friends, coworkers, bosses, and neighbors.

I once knew someone who met a prelaw student she was hell-bent on marrying. She made a point of cooking for him even when he wasn't hungry, and cleaned up after him when he got sick from too much drinking and debauchery at fraternity parties. It got to the point where he couldn't do his own laundry, and they probably got married because he couldn't get it together enough to pair his own socks.

Some people are even martyrs for their pets. I knew a woman who never went anywhere because she was sure her dogs couldn't go even a few days without her (though I think in truth it was the other way around).

It's understandable that you may be playing this part because you played it as a child. What's important now is to determine if it's something you want to continue doing as an adult. There's a good chance you don't even realize you have a choice about it.

You may find that you're forced to sit back and do less because you're exhausted or becoming physically disabled and just can't keep pushing yourself anymore. This kind of a circuit overload double bind can actually help you become less of a martyr. It forces you to establish priorities, the first of which should be yourself.

There are martyrs, however, who are more than willing to go down with the ship if that's what it takes to maintain their superiority. Those who like to be perceived as sacrificing their lives while never getting anything back are often grouchy and unhappy, no matter what others do for them.

Many individuals that have martyr characteristics may seem cheery enough while performing their family duty, but are unable to graciously accept help from those who truly care. It's as if they can "give" but can't receive. You could view them as "pathologically generous," where they tell you they are *giving*, but it feels like they are *taking*. Although giving and receiving are what make life flow and provide joy and balance, martyrs are unwilling to allow it.

If you relate to this description, be kind to yourself and give yourself credit. Since you've gotten this far in the book, you're probably motivated to change in some way. It could possibly just be a matter of not knowing how, or not giving your self permission to do so.

Hopefully, you can begin to take care of your own self in ways you never have before. It takes time and effort to allow yourself to receive help and joy from others, but it's certainly possible, no matter when and where you begin. Don't wait for others to cut you a break and take over for you. You'll have to be the one to step back and do less yourself.

Most often, the point when you begin to change is when you're circuits have overloaded. You realize then that in order to survive, you have to let something go. When you reach this decision, you're taking the first step toward escaping the martyr syndrome. Here's a story about a martyr mother who found out what happened when she finally let go.

Valerie, the Mother Who Ran Away

Valerie fumed about how her two teenage girls never listened to her. Susan, 17, was never home by her curfew, and Jennifer, 14, was always on the phone. Her son Joel, 8, could be a real sweetheart, but he, too, annoyed her by leaving the garage door open or forgetting to brush his teeth. Valerie often called from work to make sure everyone was doing what he or she was supposed to be doing. She then repeated her instructions the moment she got home.

It seemed that her words always fell on deaf ears. The kids would only listen when she finally got angry and flew into a rage. Yet, oddly, whenever something went wrong, they'd all come running to her.

As if that weren't enough, Valerie's husband, Bruce, was a disappointment. Though very good at his job at the bank, at home he never disciplined the kids or backed her up. The saddest part, which Valerie didn't let herself think about too often, was that they didn't seem to have a real relationship anymore. The only thing left was juggling bills and trying to raise the kids without totally losing it.

Valerie tried to bring this up with Bruce a number of times, but it always ended in an argument. Finally, she just gave up. She started hearing herself saying things like, "Bruce, you're as bad as the kids. If it weren't for me, absolutely nothing would get done around here. No homework would get done, Jennifer would never get off the phone, and Susan would be out all night." She knew she was only talking to herself, but it was easier than sitting in silence with no chance of any interaction at all. It never occurred to her that if he did have something to say, he wouldn't dare say it, at least not to her.

Looking back, Valerie did come to see that Bruce's silence was as much a defense against her tirades as an inability to move his lips and have a "real" discussion. However, that didn't occur to her until she discovered that the family could do pretty well without her.

Walking into the den one day, Valerie added to her usual delivery of negative redundancies by saying, "I feel like such a failure. When I picture the rest of my life, all I see is more fighting and more pain. This has got to stop!" Bruce vaguely nodded, as he always did, looking past her at the game on TV. With that, Valerie cried out, "I'm leaving!"

Bruce actually turned all the way from the TV then, and said, "Look, I'm doing the best I can. I'm just sick of hearing you complain all the time. If you really want to go, go."

Jennifer had walked into the room, and hearing her mom and dad going at it, said, "Oh, Mom, I'm off the phone now. You can use it if you want."

Valerie looked at her, burst into tears and ran out the door.

That night, she returned to pack some things, and went to stay with her sister a few hours away. The next day the kids and Bruce called and asked her to come home. Valerie told them, "No. I'm staying here for at least two weeks. You just see what it's like without me."

Valerie stuck with her decision, and by the end of the first week, said she'd come for a visit to see how things were going. When she arrived at the house, she was stunned. The place was immaculate, and the kids and Bruce had cooked dinner. She didn't know if she should laugh or cry. "Why couldn't you be like this when I'm here?" she asked.

Jennifer said, "Mom, you're so much better at everything than we are. We were never good enough for you. Please come home."

Valerie thought for a moment and said, "I'd like to, but I'm afraid that if I come home, everything will go back to the way it was. I don't know what to do."

Valerie came to my office the day after visiting her family. She kept asking, "What am I doing wrong? Why can't anyone do anything right when I'm around?"

There's nothing more excruciating than facing the fact that we are the ones getting in our own way. It's especially hard after 15 years of being seen as a nag, when all you were really trying to do was to get people to take out the trash.

I reassured Valerie that her problem is not about whether or not she was a good person. It's just that she had everyone so used to leaning on her that she finally collapsed under all the weight.

She felt reassured, and when she went home, learned to make one request of each person and made sure each one followed through. If chores weren't done exactly to her liking, she let her perfectionism go.

Over time, Valerie did less and less, as the teenage children took greater care of themselves. They also came to have more pride and accountability for the work they were assigned around the house.

I believe Valerie is still happily with the family to this day. She and her husband periodically return to my office "for maintenance" and to keep on track.

Some people continue to play the role of martyr their entire lives. Once it becomes set as a pattern, it's easy to believe it's the only way to be. Many lose hope that life could ever be better. But others step back and reevaluate whether it's something they want to keep doing. One of the trickiest aspects of martyrdom is that you may not even realize it's the role you've been playing. Perhaps you've just been so busy, you never took the opportunity to step outside the frame and see what's going on in the big picture. Try asking yourself the following questions to determine whether you've been playing the martyr role.

Are You a Martyr?

1. Have you been willing to give up your fondest dreams and goals in order to gain acceptance or love from others?

2. Do you tell yourself and others that you're tired of a given situation, yet you don't do anything to change it?

3. Do you go to extremes to be there for another family member or coworker and then wonder why it's always you who gets stuck in this position?

4. Do you avoid confrontation and then become angry and irritable later?

5. Do you ever tell yourself you're going to stop doing this for everybody, but you never do?

6. Though you may want to improve your circumstances and change your life, do you (and others) keep coming up with reasons why you must stay and keep things the way they are?

7. Do others invite you to stop doing so much, but you continue to overdo anyway, either because you feel these people would die without you, or (more honestly) that you'd lose your present identity without them?

8. Do you stay in your double-bind situation because your "uncomfortable safety zone" is at least familiar? Does living a life without feeling burdened or needed by others in constant crisis seem too foreign or risky to you?

9. Do you secretly feel you deserve better? Do you feel you're better than those who've put you in your no-win situation, even though they don't seem to think so?

10. Do you feel you care far more about other people than they ever care about you?

11. Do you feel you bend over backward for people, hoping they'll become nicer, but they only become more rude and take you more for granted?

12. Do you feel it's your lot in life to suffer, or to be the recipient of bad luck, while everyone else seems to get away with murder?

The parties involved in a martyr matrix often collude in unspoken contracts to maintain the status quo. I know a grown man who never has any adult relationships because he always "has" to travel with his family or tend to them on weekends and holidays. Just when he declares he's going to take some personal time off for himself, some family member happens to break a leg or need their hand held for some unexpected reason. Of course, there are others who could help out, but this guy always makes a point to be "Johnny on the spot" and save the day. Anyone who has the patience or stupidity to stick around and try to be this individual's lover could be called a "martyr's martyr."

People who are afraid of developing intimate, adult relationships (often called "commitment phobics") are often great candidates for becoming martyrs to their family or business. It allows them to not only avoid the anxieties of intimacy, but also props up their egos by making them feel wanted by dear old mom or dad, or sorely needed by their incapable boss. If you find yourself complaining about how you only seem to date commitment phobics, it may be that deep down you're actually one yourself. Perhaps it's *you* that's afraid of intimacy. Let's now go on to see if being the martyr in your love life is part of your no-win dilemma.

I'LL DO ANYTHING FOR LOVE
(Except for the Love Available to Me)

The main difference between the everyday martyr and the love martyr is that the love martyr rotates between moments of euphoric highs and intolerable lows around some love object of obsession. They're willing to sacrifice themselves for their ideal—and largely imagined—love. The love martyr lives under the illusion that the honeymoon period they have with someone reflects what that person can actually provide over a long period of time. The situation has all the obvious ingredients of a no-win trap, along with added drama and intense complications.

The love martyr just can't (or won't) see the red flags because their need to be in love or at least be connected is so overwhelming. The more you're willing to overlook in the beginning of a relationship, the more inclined you are to be a martyr later, when you wake up and see what you've really gotten into. This is especially so if letting go and starting over, even when the situation is intolerable, has a paralyzing and demoralizing effect on you.

The love martyr double bind is most often a reciprocal relationship: Both participants are usually acting out childhood hurts, or fears of abandonment, usually from a parent. The martyr clings to a lover who is afraid of abandonment or betrayal. The more the martyr lover clings, however, the faster and more intensely the other party pulls away, out of fear of being swallowed whole, or of being hurt or betrayed themselves.

Interestingly, and even hauntingly, the person who does the clinging in the relationship will likewise run if anyone clings to them. Thus, everyone loses in a martyr-lover double bind, as everyone is either running or clinging. The only "win" is that everyone involved gets to avoid authentic intimacy. Perhaps that's why this no-win trap is so common in our fast-paced, shallow-rooted, transient society.

Oddly enough, while martyrs complain that they don't have enough caring love and intimacy in their lives, they're amazingly unable to see how they too push it away when it willingly comes to them. They'd much rather complain about the unavailable person they're trying to "pin down," or constantly nag those who are with them about their inequities, than accept the love from someone who is actively willing to love them just as they are.

So much is said and written about people not being able to commit in relationships. However, it's not so much a matter of *whether or not* individuals are capable of being "committed," but *what they are committed to*, knowingly or unknowingly.

In the long run, martyr lovers of all sorts—whether they're running, clinging, or constantly nagging—*are more actively committed to proving there is no love for them* out there in the world than to having successful, realistic love in their lives. There's plenty of love to go around, but martyr lovers insist, as if their lives depend on it, that this is not the case.

It's probably to unconsciously prove that their parents were right in not giving them what they needed as children. There's also the possibility that their parents tried to love them the best they could, but their inadequate ways of showing it were close to the relationships martyr lovers tend to gravitate toward. Along with martyr lovers, we all have to learn to recognize and acknowledge signs of love when someone is trying to give it to us, and not go into some egocentric place where we can only recognize it when it looks like the fantasy we're desperately seeking.

Martyr lovers confuse clinging with intimacy. And those they cling to confuse the need for independence with their own fears of being abandoned or hurt if they allow themselves to receive love. Love martyrs cling as if their lives depended on it, and those they cling to tend to run away as if their lives depended on it. Those who cling to them will ultimately be left also, or be nagged to death, since the martyr must always find something wrong with those who are foolish enough to come close. They will do anything to hide the inadequacy they deny they have inside themselves.

It's no use for anyone to try to have an adult, intimate relationship with a person who runs. A truly emotionally healthy person insightfully knows not to think this behavior is because they are "not good enough." The problem is with the other person.

One of the major "hooks" that keeps a martyr lover in the game is that he or she believes the other party will stick around longer if the martyr pursuer would only lose more weight, make more money, or become more attractive in some way. However, that's often not the case. A "runner from love" is running out of habit and the often unconscious memory of emotional pain. The person who runs from a martyr lover is often a martyr for his or her own family or business. There's just no escape from the no-win when you're either clinging or running. The only way to overcome it is to find the courage to verbally negotiate what it is you need and what you don't want.

Love martyrs double-bind themselves, at least in part, because they believe the other party is actually capable of being attached to them in some healthy and intimate way—when in truth they aren't. What they are is expert at giving the impression that there's hope. If you're a love martyr, you know what I mean. They always seem to know just when to throw you a bone—when you're right on the verge of leaving.

Most likely, part of the problem is the way you go about looking for love and what you perceive is good for you. It could be you're trying to do the right thing with the wrong people. They might at first look like they want to engage in a long-term and loving relationship with you, but can be that way only until you get "too close." Then they're suddenly a lot less available, or they want to be with someone else (especially if that someone is also not available).

All no-win situations make you feel you're damned if you do and damned if you don't, but when it comes to the martyr lover double bind, there are a number of special aspects. First, let's look at the basic issues this no-win trap has in common with others:

- You feel trapped by a conflict or problem. You're convinced you can neither escape nor win the battle. (Concerning being a martyr lover, you can't live with them and you can't live without them.)

- Despite this, you feel compelled or have a strong sense of responsibility to do something to solve the problem. (A martyr lover is obsessively determined to make the relationship "work." Whether you're trying to get a person to be more in your life or insisting that someone should see and do things your way, you are forcing an issue that is not working in your favor.)

- You believe you can't have a successful conversation with the person you need to talk to the most. That person is convinced—or acts like they're convinced—that the problem lies entirely with you. Approaching them only seems to make matters worse. (The martyr lover is unsuccessful in having a conversation that helps the situation. Or if there has been what seems a useful conversation, the follow-up behavior in no way reflects what was said.)

Martyr lover double binds also have one or more of the following additional, unique components:

- You feel there's a chance for love if only you hang in there long enough and somehow "do the right thing." You have the idea this is all about *you*. It doesn't occur to you that instead of your inadequacies, the other party doesn't have what it takes to have a successful relationship with anybody.

- Even though there may be other opportunities for love, you believe this person is the only one for you.

- Your self-esteem is suffering in the process, but you don't really care (even though you may complain about it). It's your low self-esteem that got you into this jam—if you loved yourself better, you'd have never gone looking for love here in the first place.

- You think you'll be devastated and hurt if you leave. However, deep down you know that if you stay, you eventually will be hurt and devastated even more. There's something romantically familiar about all this.

- You can't discuss the issue to your satisfaction with the other party and feel frustrated each time you try. In reality, your whining or "discussions" only blind you further. You pretend to buy into what the other person is saying, when you know deep down you'll only be disappointed one more time.

- You may even be afraid or feel unworthy of verbalizing any needs you have for your own well-being.

- The closer you both come toward some sort of intimacy, the more the other person pushes away. You could be double-binding the other person as much as he or she seems to be doing with you.

- Other people could become involved, creating a triangle, and yet you still feel there's a way you can "win," or at least you still believe there's something in it for you.

- The martyr lover double bind can become an addiction. The situation can go from wonderful to horrific in a very short amount of time. This pattern can be repeated over and over, accompanied by long-winded soliloquies about how you're finally breaking up and are never going back to the relationship again.

- You could also have a pattern of backing off from a relationship that turns out to go well, and you're frightened that it "could be too good to be true." Without realizing it, you reject the other person before they get a chance to reject you.

Now let's look at how these principles play out in the following case.

Susan and Her Lost Love

Susan, a woman I know, told me she believed she could make Richard, the man she had been seeing, happy enough to finalize his pending divorce and leave his wife and two teenage children. Susan first met Richard on a commuter train into New York City. He told her he had left his family six months earlier because he was sick and tired of hearing his wife complain when he got home late after working hard every day and accuse him of really being out with other women. Besides, he had planned to leave her when the kids were out of the house anyway, so he didn't feel bad about his decision.

Susan listened intently, meanwhile thinking that she could be a "better fit" for this man than his wife, since she often worked late too. She really felt sorry for him. Susan threw herself into the relationship. While Richard was very attentive to her enough in the beginning, he became more and more preoccupied as time went on. She overlooked the fact that "Mr. Wonderful" constantly spoke of his wife and children, complaining about them on the one hand and missing them on the other. She also ignored the fact that the telephone kept ringing whenever she went to visit her new beau late at night and on weekends. Richard explained that it was his kids calling him for money or to handle some situation that happened at home or school.

Susan was now caught in a troubling double bind. She didn't want to lose Richard, but she also didn't want to have to deal with his increasing moodiness whenever the phone rang. When Susan finally brought this up, Richard tried to calmly assure her he would handle it. He told her he decided he would go back for a week or two to the house where his (supposedly) separated wife and kids lived to try and clear up a few issues. He told Susan she could stay at his apartment as often as she liked, and he'd come back as soon as he took care of "everything." It's amazing how readily we overlook the obvious when we desperately want to. Evidently, Susan had more of a need to stay in this relationship than to have peace in her life. She accepted Richard's answer and stayed on.

A long and arduous six months later, after Richard would sporadically come back to his apartment to see her for "a romantic rendezvous," Susan finally realized that Richard had been living a double life and probably had never really left his wife and kids. Susan eventually left and moved on, but it took her a long time to mend her broken heart.

Down the road, she met another man, Charles. Life, as it tends to, was apparently giving her the opportunity to see if she'd learned her lesson. When she went to visit him, she noticed that the phone kept ringing and he never picked it up. Finally he admitted, "That's my 'old flame,' but it's over and we're not seeing each other anymore. She just keeps calling me to see if I'll come back."

This time Susan stated right off the bat: "From the sound of your phone, you're not available. Even though you say you are, the other party apparently hasn't fully gotten the message. I won't be able to see you, and I'll let myself out."

It had taken an emotional roller-coaster ride and a threatening situation for her to learn her lesson. Susan had successfully removed herself from what would have been another tortuous and complicated no-win situation.

Some people, of course, never catch on, no matter how problematic circumstances become. Many people who see an inkling of love or a crumb of affection are quick to declare that this is the romance they've been waiting for all their lives. Too often they're willing to stay on for a long time—sometimes even forever—struggling to turn that crumb into a five-course dinner.

All of this is done in the name of so-called love. But most often the reason is to convince ourselves that we're not alone. Even if there isn't an "ex" in the scene, we pretend we're having a relationship with an "available" person, when in truth we're only spinning our wheels and are still very much on our own. Consider the following real life story. See if you recognize some part of yourself.

Laverne Hangs On

Laverne just couldn't believe it. At the age of 43, after having been married and divorced two times, she had finally found Mr. Right, a man just two years younger than she. She met Michael through an Internet dating service and had gone out with him several times. The relationship felt almost too good to be true. It seemed they had everything in common, including teenage children the same age.

She'd begun the process slowly at first, as she'd been advised. They played bridge and went out to dinner twice a month. While there was a developing attraction, no sexual come-ons had yet taken place. Laverne was thoroughly intrigued with the man, a prosperous Web site business owner. He could talk for hours at a time, and she held onto every word. She found him fascinating, and he reminded her of everything she adored about her father. As her dear old dad had also had his downside, Laverne was aware that trouble might loom ahead, but she set her concerns aside and merrily went on with what she thought was a developing romance.

Soon, however, Michael began to call her less and less. After some bouts of frustration, Laverne finally started dating other people. But somehow this just made her miss Michael even more. In fact, the kinder and more attentive the other guys were, the less interested she was. It appeared that no one but Michael would do. Laverne did find, however, that this other dating in some odd way was worth her while. Michael seemed to sense when she was drifting away from him, and then she'd get a call from him again.

This sporadic contact continued for months. It seemed that as long as Laverne wasn't focused exclusively on Michael, he would call and they'd go out on a semiregular basis.

Then Laverne went away on a two-week vacation. Michael called and left messages at her home. Laverne returned one of them and left some of the numbers where she was staying with friends and relatives. Michael called all of them, just missing her by hours each time.

Laverne came to see that Michael liked the chase. As long as she ran fast enough for him not to catch her, the race was on. If she made herself available, Michael pulled back.

When Laverne returned home, Michael made a big deal about taking her out to celebrate her promotion at work. That night they finally became romantically entangled. Michael could not have been more attentive. And over the next month or so, he called her almost every day, and they saw each other once or twice a week. Laverne now had the impression that they were in a budding relationship, and she looked forward to dating on a regular basis.

It was not to be. After one of the most romantic evenings either of them had ever experienced, Michael began to make himself scarce. He told her he was "stepping up his business plans and had some difficult issues to iron out." That should have been a sign to Laverne that he was afraid of getting too close, but she kept on seeing him whenever she could.

Another week went by, and Michael left another message on her machine that his business and entire financial and emotional condition was even worse than he'd thought it would be. Laverne really felt for him and hung in like a saint. A month went by without a word, and then Laverne called Michael to say she was thinking of him. He said he was glad to hear from her and would call her by the end of that week.

The call never came. In fact, it wasn't until a month later that she finally heard from him again. He asked her out to dinner, and Laverne promptly went. Afterward, they fell into each other's arms like never before. Michael even commented on how wonderful she felt and that it seemed as if "it just keeps getting better and better." When he left later that evening, he told her he'd had a wonderful time and mumbled something about getting in touch.

Christmas went by without a call. New Year's went by. No call. Finally, Laverne decided she'd had enough. When he finally called and suggested they get together on January 15, she hung up on him.

Looking back, Laverne had learned an important lesson about how much of a martyr she had become in this relationship, and noted how often she'd acted similarly in the past. She promised she would never allow herself to fall into that trap again.

What about you? Can you relate? How low are you willing to stoop for a measly crumb of so-called love? Do you run from someone who's willing and able to love you well, but run far away when you're getting too close?

Whether you relate to only one or all of the points that follow, you may have some aspect of the martyr lover in your life. Be kind to yourself and not self-critical if you see yourself here. Everyone is doing the best they can in giving and receiving in relationships. The more you're just willing to observe what is *really* happening in your life, the closer you'll be to the real happiness and satisfaction you deserve.

Are You a Martyr for Love?

1. Do you find yourself constantly thinking about this individual or trying to show you care, while he or she comes across as if you aren't terribly important to them? Do you sometimes wonder if perhaps this relationship is more a figment of your imagination than a real connection or commitment? Do you spend more time pondering the potential of where this could possibly go than where it is right now?

   The martyr lover is often consumed with a picture of an idealistic relationship that is not possible with the particular person in question. Make sure you aren't trying to do the "right" thing with the "wrong" person.

2. Do you find yourself starting out enthusiastically wanting to be with someone, only to find they aren't as appealing to you

the more they return the feeling? Whether you're the one who withholds love or unsuccessfully craves it, you're tangled up in the martyr-lover syndrome one way or another.

The martyr lover can find him- or herself in the no-win trap of being able to give but not being able to receive. It takes a willingness to give up control sometimes when you're open and willing to receive from another person and begin sharing who you are and what you need. The martyr lover often wants to give the impression of not needing anyone and being totally independent, not realizing a healthy relationship needs "interdependence."

3. The martyr lover is often inclined to have more compassion and empathy for the needs and behavior of the other person than for him- or herself. While they may appear saintlike, it could be due to the fact that the martyr lover's low self-esteem will justify and support anything to stay in the game. It's one thing to do anything for love. It's quite another to do anything to avoid being alone.

4. Do you find yourself noticing the one you love seems to treat everyone else with more regard than you?

5. Do you find the nicer and more caring you are, the more they take you for granted? And if they do finally call you after a long silence and you don't jump, then they're either mad or chase you for a while? It seems they only do just enough to keep you in the game. They want you waiting on the shelf, but not actively in their life.

Another way of putting it is, do you ever feel your partner doesn't really want you, but they don't want anyone else to have you either? I know of a woman who only gets attention from her husband in public when he wants to look like a nice guy, or wants to make sure no one else offers her a drink or a decent conversation.

6. Do you find you're kinder to those you are trying to connect with than those who are "easily obtainable"? A good way to see

as many angles as possible concerning the martyr lover is to consider the possibility that you may take others for granted the way someone you love may be treating you. Without realizing it, martyr lovers can single-mindedly focus on those they don't already have in their corner, and forget to nurture the solid relationships they do have.

Be especially kind to yourself if you recognize any of the double-bind responses outlined in this chapter. As we've noted, many of these negative behaviors were learned in childhood. The good news is, it's never too late to "unlearn" what doesn't work for you. This doesn't require making you or anyone else the "bad guy." It's only important that you look back at your life to see how early double binds have influenced your thinking. We'll explore this further in Chapter 5, but for now, turn to Chapter 4 to examine how you're doing overall in life and how you're dealing with your no-win dilemmas.

Hang in there. Help is in sight. Finding the way out of difficult problems is part of the journey of life. Hopefully, this challenging process will bring us home to ourselves. Then, and only then, will we be able to fully relate to others without losing ourselves again.

4

How Double-Binded Are You?

Pain is meant to be a messenger, not a roommate.

Paul Ferrini

Let's take a closer look at your own life and examine just how much has been determined by your internal thoughts and attitudes, rather than by external circumstances. While it may appear that the no-win traps in which you find yourself were caused by external circumstances and other people, they were in fact caused by your own responses to situations presented to you.

Rather than inviting you to feel like a blamed victim of circumstance, the above statements are intended to help you see just how powerful you really are! Consider these additional concepts:

- Your thinking and attitudes about yourself and others will have a direct influence on how you respond to life situations.

- Your own beliefs about yourself influence the way others will perceive you.

- In fact, your beliefs, thinking, and attitudes directly determine which kinds of people and situations are drawn to you.

YOUR THINKING AND ATTITUDES

Over time, if you don't check in with yourself regularly—as so many of us fail to do—and examine underlying feelings about situations and the various options available to you, your beliefs and attitudes can become frozen in place, creating a kind of emotional coma. Without realizing it, you can lock yourself into the same, recurring response to life, and thus fail to consider more rewarding approaches. It's like casting yourself in one role in a play and staying with it forever.

Look back and consider how often you've said the following things to yourself or others:

- "I can't believe this always happens to me!" (Of course, the more you say this, the more you'll come to believe it.)

- "I never get what I want." (You can become so familiar with not getting what you want that eventually you come to expect it.)

- "Other people are so lucky." (This effectively undercuts your responsibility for doing all you can to be who you're meant to be. We often use this line to give up on ourselves.)

- "Every time my life starts to go well, something goes wrong to screw it up." (That's a tough belief to get over. The truth is, life doesn't have to be that way—unless it's your built-in expectation.)

- "Of course I had to do what I did. I had no other option." (At the moment it may have appeared that way, but options are almost always available.)

This sort of thinking guarantees that you'll be stuck in no-win traps, or be attracted to them. Uncovering these inner and outer conversations will help give you more insight into the nature of your double binds.

YOUR BELIEFS INFLUENCE HOW OTHERS SEE YOU

Think how often you've said any of these:

- "I don't get it. My boss is nice to everyone but me." (It's likely that you come across in a way that makes your boss feel he can mistreat you. This doesn't make his mistreatment "right"; it just means that you appear to be someone who'll put up with that mistreatment.)

- "I get stuck doing all the chores in this house. Everyone treats me like the maid." (Patterns are hard to change. Perhaps everyone is so accustomed to seeing you do everything that they no longer think they need to help. Or perhaps you're such a perfectionist that you've convinced everyone they could never do things as well as you.)

- "Every time we go out, all the guys want to talk to my girlfriend, but they never talk to me." (You may have designated yourself to be a sidekick rather than the person who is out to meet new people. If others have cast you in that part, perhaps you've willingly taken on the role in order to continue to be with these people.)

- "Every time I apply for a job, I get a second interview, but I never land the position." (Someone is getting that job. What message do you give about yourself?)

Remember that none of this is about blame or criticism. It's about trying to uncover the hidden patterns that are keeping you from playing out a winning role in your life.

YOUR BELIEFS AND ATTITUDES DIRECTLY DETERMINE WHAT IS DRAWN TO YOU

While it may initially sound like magical mumbo jumbo, it makes perfect sense that your own actual beliefs (or at least whatever you buy into at any given time) would directly determine which kinds of people and situations are magnetized toward your direction. Like-minded people, whether consciously or unconsciously, are bound to find each other. It's no secret that if you are drunk at a party, you'll be inclined to attract different individuals and experiences from those you'd come across if you were sober. (You'll also get different responses from those you come across.)

Remember the cliques in junior high and high school? It's rather amusing to think the same kinds of groupings and the same sorts of behaviors take place at almost every school to some degree, even if the students never do meet those from other places. The rest of our lives actually involve being placed in various types of groupings almost the same way, although it is much less obvious.

Consider the following statements. Perhaps you've found yourself saying or feeling some of them:

- "How come I always seem to attract all the losers, while my girlfriend always gets all the good guys?" (While you may believe you think a lot of yourself, perhaps some unrealized low self-esteem pattern or need to seem "better" than those around you propels you to attract those you are inclined to want to reject or put down in some way.)

- "I don't know how he does it! He always manages to surround himself with good people." (This could be a sign of a person with a lot of integrity and wisdom who knows how to attract the right people. On the other hand, this could be an individual with a personality disorder that allows him to know what to say and how to say it to individuals who are basically good people but who have some hidden flaw in their character that sets them up to be taken. Quite often, that flaw is the overcompensating need to please others, even if it jeopardizes themselves.)

- "I'm tired of always attracting people who take advantage of me." (This could potentially be a martyr who makes a living pretending not to see the red flags at first and then overly pointing them out to others later.)

- "I can't get over how well my day always seems to go whenever I wear this dress!" (The saying "You're only as good as you feel" isn't far off the mark.)

- "I seem to go a long time without meeting anyone new. Then, all of a sudden, I meet a lot of new people all at once." (It's amazing how the whole world seems to know when you are open to new energy and when you're not.)

- "I can't get over how the women all flock to me now that I have a girlfriend and I'm no longer looking. Before I met my fiancé, I couldn't seem to catch a cold." (While it's true that most people are often attracted to someone who is happy and confident, in this particular scenario, chances are that the people who would be attracted to someone in a committed relationship are the ones who would most likely not be interested in someone who is available or attracted to them. If you find yourself *always* drawn to those who are unavailable, that could mean you are more "wired" to go after someone you can't get than you are to receive someone who could actually have a relationship with you.)

- "The bar in that restaurant always seems to attract a down and out sort of clientele." (It is interesting to note how one place can be "inviting" to some people while the same place can represent "Danger! Do not enter!" to others.)

Read on. This chapter is designed to help you gain more insight concerning how your core beliefs set you up to get the life you have even more than the other way around.

COGNITIVE STRESS MANAGEMENT SCALE

The self-rating process set out below is designed to help you examine the ways you view your life. As you read through and answer the questions, try to be as honest as you can without becoming critical or laying blame. Improvement starts the moment you're able to see yourself clearly.

What's Your Happiness Quotient?

How happy are you with your life right now? From the happiness quotient scale below, choose the one number that most closely describes the way you feel. If you feel you're at different numbers for different issues in your life, that's perfectly understandable. For the purpose of this exercise, however, choose the one that most reflects how life in general feels to you in this moment.

The results will give you an idea of how much you need to change your life in order to move up the happiness scale to a number you most want your life to reflect. Keep this in mind as you read through the rest of the book, exploring various ways to move your happiness quotient higher.

10.   You are happy and could remain so in this circumstance for a very long time. You choose to see the difficult moments as normal by-products of life. You're able to discern when to make changes in your life as the need arises. Your insight concerning when to make decisions comes easily.

9.   Once in a while you're faced with a daunting dilemma, but you say and do what's necessary to your general satisfaction. You recognize life has curveballs, and you recuperate quickly. When something doesn't go as you'd expect, you have the ability to isolate the issues involved, rather than believing that you're losing everything.

8.   There are a few long-term or long-range problems that you feel in your gut need to be addressed. Despite some apprehension, you accomplish your objectives sooner rather than later. You recognize that these situations should be handled in a timely manner to prevent them from becoming larger or overwhelming.

7.   More often than you care to admit, you bite your tongue or lower your standards. You tell yourself things are okay because other options look even more unattractive. Others seem to have it worse than you do, so you tell yourself, "At least I'm not as bad off as they are." You know you're not as happy as you'd like to be, but you convince yourself that things are okay, at least for now.

6.   You wonder if this is all life has in store for you. You feel that your life or your important relationships are flat, boring, annoying, or just "not as good as they used to be." Life often seems like ongoing drudgery. You keep hoping things will improve, but you're not sure how that will come about. You wonder if all this is even worth your effort. Part of the problem is that while there's not enough joy to make you happy,

there's not enough overt "pain" to prompt you to make major changes. Be careful not to settle in and stay here.

5. You're angry and hurt. You have knee-jerk reactions to an uncomfortable degree. This is a good time to detach and see what you're adding to the problem, but you find this extremely difficult to do. You're so focused on what the other players in this situation are doing that you can't see your own part. If you could have one moment of clear insight, however, you'd have a chance to move up the scale.

   If anger is besieging you, be careful. Anger is often employed to "rally the troops" to doing something to improve the situation, or at least to alter it in some way. The problem is that anger is often unconsciously used to blame others for your circumstances. If you're not careful, you could put all your energy into blaming someone else, and have none left to actually do something to improve your situation.

4. This is where depression, headaches, insomnia, and inability to concentrate kick in. You begin to drown in your sorrows, or mask them in some way. A negative habit can set in, where you fall into regressive behavior. Addictive or avoiding behaviors could keep you from feeling the full extent of your pain. It's important to get help here, if you haven't already, before long-term, negative patterns set in.

3. Almost every day at least one dilemma is thrust in front of you in the form of a confrontation or new problematic development. It takes everything and then some to hang on. Somehow you do manage to hang on, but you don't know how long you can last.

2. You find yourself saying, "I give up. I don't care anymore." As low as this number is on the scale, it's actually an improvement over a 3 *if* you can recognize it more as an opportunity than a crisis. Sometimes things have to get this bad before you're finally able to let go and allow yourself new perspectives you've never considered before.

Hopefully, at this point, you're more open to advice than ever before. If you're not usually inclined to ask for help, you may see it as a possibility now. Conversely, if you're at this number on the scale and you're still convinced you know what you're doing, you're unwittingly committed to your no-win trap.

1. Spiraling down to this point, an external or internal crash of some sort comes ironically to "save the day." This is where no matter how much you've tried to keep going while being pulled in all directions, the power and momentum of one direction finally wins out over the others. The situation you were in falls apart, making the decision for you. There's no turning back now. The good news, if there is any, is that you get to see what the bottom looks like: Hopefully, if at this point you choose to face where you really are, allow yourself to get real help, and commit to improving your stance on life from here on out, it may not have to get any worse than this. Clarity, new solutions, better perspectives and insight could be just around the corner. For now, however, it's perfectly understandable if all you feel is pain. Make no attempt to do all this alone. Let others be there for you like never before.

If you're currently at 8, 9, or 10—what I call the "high happiness" range—try to make this a lifestyle rather than only an occasional occurrence. If you're in the middle ground of 5, 6, or 7, don't wait for things to get worse, at which point you'll be forced to make drastic changes. Be proactive. Move up the scale while you still have the energy.

If you're down around 1 through 4, ask yourself, "How long will I let myself suffer before I finally decide to get help?" If you've learned to expect to live with pain all your life, you could come to mistake it as your only friend.

In reality, when you are willing and brave enough to meet "head-to-head" with your pain, you'll be inclined to face your issues directly and take action to improve your situation, hopefully for the long run. When you do not deal directly with your pain, you end up sinking down further and further in your dilemma, losing ground and losing hope. When the situation is not tolerable and you don't make effective changes, the circumstance takes over. You could then settle in for some long-term suffering.

People often consider "pain" and "suffering" to be one and the same. They're not. While the dictionary seems to mention them interchangeably, it also equates pain with distress and suffering with misery. Distress can be seen as an acute sign, telling you that something is not right and something needs to be done. Misery, on the other hand, reeks of eternal doom. The pain you face today saves you the suffering that's waiting for you tomorrow.

When you feel your condition is too much to handle, when you aren't sure you can even go on, you must accept that the pain is not meant to be dealt with alone. Let others be there for you. They may help you tap into sources of strength you never knew you had.

A new way of life is always available when the time is right for you to see it. As Marcel Proust so eloquently put it: "The real voyage of discovery consists not in seeking new landscapes but in having new eyes."

We know that inner beliefs form the foundation of perception. Your experiences are interpreted within the framework of these beliefs, and from that interpretation comes your response. With this in mind, let's examine carefully your current view of life. Be as honest as you can with your answers.

MY PRESENT VIEW OF LIFE

Self-Rating Scale

Answer the following true and false questions. Circle the number next to the true or false. If you feel the answer is not 100 percent true, then mark false.

1. There definitely is a way for me to succeed
   in life.   True - 2   False - 1

2. I truly feel joy in my life.   True - 2   False - 1

3. I know I am forgiven when I make
   mistakes.   True - 2   False - 1

4. There is no doubt I will accomplish
   my dreams.   True - 2   False - 1

5. Life is really good, and I know there are
   issues I need to work on. I know where
   to start, and I'll get to them sooner
   rather than later.   True - 2   False - 1

6. Even though I know doing everything at
   the last minute is stressful for myself
   and others, I seem to do it anyway.   True - 1   False - 2

7. I believe I have good boundaries with
   people and know what I can be responsible
   for and what I can't. I know when to
   say yes and when to say no.   True - 2   False - 1

8. There are times when I feel like blaming
   others for my problems, but I know
   assigning blame won't help me deal
   with things effectively.   True - 2   False - 1

9. I wish life could be better, but I'm
   coasting along.   True - 1   False - 2

10. I keep hoping things will just get better,
    but I'm afraid they probably won't.   True - 1   False - 2

11. I am a good person, but I feel bad things
    happen to me often.   True - 1   False - 2

12. It's often hard to get a good night's sleep,
    since I worry about what I have to face
    the next day.   True - 1   False - 2

13. Life just isn't what I had hoped it would be. True - 1   False - 2

14. I don't know how I feel. I just know life isn't
    much fun. I'm tired of taking care of every-
    body else; no one ever takes care of me.   True - 1   False - 2

15. Even though I know what I should do about
    my life, I hardly ever seem to do it.   True - 1   False - 2

16. I find myself feeling hurt and angry because
    of other people in my life. Sometimes I feel
    they're out to get me.   True - 1   False - 2

17. Life would be so much easier if people just
    did things my way.   True - 1   False - 2

18. Almost everyone has it easier than I do.
    Nothing comes easy for me.   True - 1   False - 2

19. Maybe if I just keep going, I'll win the
    lottery or something and others will
    leave me alone.   True - 1   False - 2

20. No matter what I do, every day is a struggle.
    Often it's the same thing over and over
    again. I don't know how much more
    I can take.   True - 1   False - 2

21. No matter how hard I try, I can't seem
    to please anyone.   True - 1   False - 2

22. Everything is so overwhelming. I wish
    someone would help me, but I don't even
    know where to begin to ask for help.   True - 1   False - 2

23. If only I could go back and change my
    past, my life would be better today.   True - 1   False - 2

24. This is the worst my life has ever been, and
    I feel I'm stuck here for good.   True - 1   False - 2

25. I know that no matter how I answered this
    survey, as long as I'm honest with myself
    and willing to be responsible for where I
    am in life, I'm going to be okay.   True - 2   False - 1

Hopefully, the very act of answering these questions has inspired you to think about your life and how things in general are going. If you're concerned about your answers, the good news is you're being honest with yourself. When you begin to clearly see your underlying thinking, you can begin to understand its effect on your life, in terms of both your own responses and those of the people around you. The more you begin to question your thinking and work to improve your beliefs and attitudes, the more fully you can engage in a healthy life, no matter who or what you're confronted with.

For now, add up your total score and then read below to see how much or how little you're inclined to fall into a no-win trap. Notice that there is some overlap in the points and what they mean. If your total score falls into two different categories of explanations, decide which one best describes how your life is going now.

44 to 50 Points: Congratulations! You're someone who is very self-aware and can tap into what's going on with other people. You see mistakes as lessons to be learned and problems as opportunities for change. You avoid no-win traps wherever possible, and you learn from the ones you've been in. You also see self-responsibility as a privilege, and a sign that you can be responsive to life, rather than as a drudgery or burden. This would correlate to 9 to 10 on the Cognitive Stress Management Scale earlier in the chapter.

36 to 44 Points: Life is probably going pretty well most of the time. You have a fairly honest and positive relationship with reality, and you handle the curveballs quite well. You may want to consider taking on new experiences and risks to see if life has more in store. While being careful not to overshoot your goals, you also shouldn't settle for less than you deserve. Make sure you're truly happy. Don't mistake complacency for genuine fulfillment. It's good to take time to smell the roses, but make sure you're not just coasting along. This would correlate with a 7 to 8 on the Cognitive Stress Management Scale.

32 to 36 Points: Falling into this range means it's time to get help. Don't wait any longer for the situation or for other people to change. It's important not to get bogged down with blaming yourself or others. It only steals energy from you and keeps you from recognizing what's necessary to improve your life.

If anger or hurt comes easily to you, it could be a sign that you're unaware of the part you play in your problems. If you feel you don't have your needs met because you're taking care of everyone else's, make sure you're not so used to giving out energy to others that you don't give others the chance to give back to you. Be careful not to be cynical that you have no one to lean on.

It's easy to attract people who'll prove you're right, when deep down you're just afraid of being disappointed one more time. Choose those who can actually come through so you don't double-bind yourself by insisting they change when they haven't in the past. Also, don't double-bind others by making sure there's no way that they can win with you either.

This would correlate to 4, 5, and 6 on the CSM Scale. If you feel you've been barraged by double binds in your life, this is the part of the scale where scapegoats, fix-it people, and those who "hang around for the carrot" tend to live. Martyrs could also find themselves here, especially if they accept their position as a way of life.

25 to 32 Points: This correlates to 1, 2, and 3 on the CSM Scale. Falling into this category means it's time to seriously consider making major changes in your life. It probably seems like life itself is the problem, but the real problem lies in the way you're responding. You need help and insight to face what's actually going on. Try not to beat up on yourself. Make this your "bottom line," without going any lower. Slow down and take care of your own needs first. This is no time to keep trying to please people who seem impossible to please.

If you're down this low, and you believe yourself to be a scapegoat, fix-it person, or martyr of some sort, consider these low numbers as a sign that it is time to stop trying to hold everything up on your own two cylinders. Let go and see where the chips fall. Get help in effectively taking care of your needs, and consider getting good insight from others to help you see what you can do with your situation and what you can't.

There is no way to change the past, and your future will only be the same if you insist on doing things the same way you're doing them now. Let others be there for you in ways you haven't in the past. Life is overwhelming when you don't let other people in on what's going on. This is no time to look as if you have it all together when you really don't.

The more you commit yourself to improving your life, doing whatever it takes in any single moment, the higher you'll raise your "bottom line" and the higher you'll live on the happiness scale. Self-determination can catalyze us to reach deep inside ourselves and find the strength to get through situations we never dreamed we could. You must trust that this inner resource is there. You need only to be willing to find it.

5

Breaking Your Patterns
of Dissatisfaction

What lies behind us and what lies before us are tiny matters, compared to what lies within us.

Ralph Waldo Emerson

*A*fter all is said and done, all no-win traps lead back to the one original and ultimate double bind that hurts us the most: being afraid that life will pass us by without the love, acceptance, and accomplishment we've always wanted. At the same time, we may be unable to trust or receive the love, acceptance, and accomplishment we already have. Our career, marriage, relationships, or opportunities may not be working out in the way we'd always hoped. We may not be exactly sure what it is that's going wrong, but we're plagued with a nagging sense of chronic dissatisfaction.

If you're facing this sort of dissatisfaction, it's time to take an honest look at yourself. You may have unwittingly lived your life always falling short of your dreams. Without realizing it, you could be pushing away real possibilities for love and success that are right in front of you, while believing that you have no access to what it is you really want. Or perhaps you don't know what you really want, and you expect those around you to figure it out for you. Or perhaps you have a habit of attracting people and situations that only perpetuate the negative or conflicting beliefs you've developed about how life will be for you.

In this chapter we'll examine your patterns of dissatisfaction, and help you turn those patterns around. We'll do this by looking deeply into your core experiences—those building blocks of your psyche assembled in your childhood.

The years of a person's life come and go, and trailing along with them are memories and events that influence our beliefs. In his book, *Childhood and Society*, Erik Erikson talks about the eight developmental stages of man. Stage eight, Dignity versus Despair, covers the later years, when a person is reviewing his or her overall life. When you reach that point, will you look back with a feeling of dignity, or will your evaluation bring up only thoughts of despair?

For many of us, the saddest prospect would be to never experience the "love of a lifetime," a relationship with that special someone who absolutely adored and cared for us just as we are. Equally important—if not more so—is the potential tragedy of never coming to terms with fully loving yourself just the way you are.

We've all read or heard it said that no one else can ever love you more than you truly love yourself. Yet it's so easy to deceive yourself, to act as if you're focused and satisfied when you really aren't, to try to persuade yourself and the world to think you're someone you're not. You end up actually deceiving those who do want to get close.

It's a self-fulfilling prophecy. If you don't believe that others will accept your true Self, then you're not giving them the person you really are. And if you don't give others who you really are, there's no way they can ever truly love and accept the real you.

And when you realize that jobs, relationships, marriages, and other situations aren't what you thought they were, you in turn begin to feel that *you've* been deceived.

In this self-fulfilling prophecy of self-deception, you can get so far from trying to please yourself that you end up by trying to overly please others. These excessive efforts to please others are often a way of "overempowering" them to the point of disempowering yourself. It gives the other person unspoken free reign to treat you any way they choose, because you've made the mistake of thinking their opinion of you is more important than your own. Essentially, you're giving them the power to mistreat you. If you refuse to "hold your own," there's a good chance you won't like the way others hold it for you. While you're likely to find many individuals who seem delighted to run your life, in the long run they'll feel overburdened and will grow to resent you. And you, in turn, will resent them.

The most important and helpful way to cut through this self-deception and imbalance in power is to take a detached but compassionate look at the roles you play in your life. Are you effectively going after the things you really want? Do good people and situations seem to come your way? Do things generally work out? Are you being genuine? Try to answer these questions as honestly as you can. You can then understand how you've set the stage and how others play into their "scenes" with you.

It's important to get to a place where you can accept yourself even if others don't. Only in that way can you be ready to move on when you need to, and to accept positive occurrences without questioning whether they're "too good to be true."

Do you feel you hardly ever have your own needs met, or that you have to try harder than others to achieve any satisfaction? Or do you believe success can realistically be yours? The sooner you understand how your past helped create your current double binds, the sooner you'll be able to move out of them toward a life of possibility and long-term satisfaction.

THE FOUNDATIONS OF NO-WIN TRAPS

For those who seem to be the most unhappy or whose lives are most conflicted, there are three basic types of no-win traps that have usually occurred in their childhood. They form the infernal fountainhead from which all other double binds are created:

1. Feeling that you're never good enough, yet believing you're too good for what you already have

2. Believing that everyone but you gets what they want, and what you get is always second best

3. The conviction that you have to do everything yourself, and what you get in return never measures up

Where do these primal no-win traps and woebegotten assumptions come from? How do they get started? And what can you do to break through their barriers to find freedom, love, and genuine self-acceptance?

We'll examine these three no-win traps at length in this chapter. Consider them with great love for yourself and those around you.

NO-WIN TRAP I
You're Never Good Enough, but You're Too Good for What You Have

Those stuck in this no-win trap may find themselves saying or thinking:

"I'm afraid to make anyone mad."

"I've got to be the one to save the day, or they'll never accept me."

"No matter how hard I try, I never do anything right."

"How come there are no good men out there?"

"I want a woman who won't try to change me."

"There are no good jobs out there."

"I never get what I want."

"I deserve so much more than this."

"I have so much to do before I'm even close to being acceptable."

Breaking Free of No-Win Trap I

In this no-win trap, you feel you never get the love and acceptance you long for, while believing the apparent love and acceptance you do get is not good enough for you. While you almost always think you "deserve better," you're constantly haunted by the underlying thought that you may not *ever* be good enough. While you despise yourself for settling, you don't have the inner resources to move on.

When you do come across a great opportunity for love or self-expression, you find ways to sabotage it or make it wrong for you. Without realizing it, you actually feel "safer" being a rejecting fish in the wrong pond, even if you've outgrown it to the point of annoying those who will always be stuck there. It's the familiarity that keeps you there. When you refuse to grow and let go, the chances of becoming a scapegoat or ostracized increase. Yet you remain connected to them for some reason, as if you're "protected," or at least know the game.

Complications increase when midlife looms and you're haunted by thoughts of missed opportunities and lost chances for love. Although there may even be times when you do venture out, if you came from a childhood where your spirit was broken and you didn't develop the roots to feel safe and secure, the fear of being put down or rejected is enough to muster up a "good reason" to not be as wonderful as you truly could be.

Below is a case of a woman who was so confused she couldn't decide if the love she lost was the chance of a lifetime, or if she was better off leaving. What she does discover is that although she was looking for someone to love and accept her, she was actually looking to accept herself.

Ellen's Confusion about Love and Life

Ellen grew up with her younger sister Gwen and her cousin Paul, who lived with her family. Her sister always seemed to have problems that demanded their parents' constant attention. And although her mother had a degree in fine arts from a prestigious art school, Mom blamed herself and her family for having never done much with it.

Ellen enrolled in art class, and her teacher soon noted how well she was doing. But no matter how hard Ellen worked in art school or anywhere else, she was always shot down at home. She either had to hear about how Dad always thought Paul was the best tennis player in the family, or how proud Mom was when her sister Gwen came home with a one-handed puppet she'd made in school, or something else congratulatory that she herself hadn't done. In fact, the more she showed the others up, the more she was ignored or belittled.

The only time Ellen felt that she got any attention was when she went to work with her dad, helping him with his real estate business. When the two of them walked to his office, she felt wonderful and accepted, and wished that the feeling could continue when they were back home.

One day, Ellen asked her father why Mom always let Gwen have her own way. He looked down at her lovingly and, for the only time Ellen could remember, came to her defense. "I know what you mean," he told her. "Sometimes I feel Mom gets mad at me too, for being so frustrated with Gwen, and for being mad at how she always gives in to her."

Ellen couldn't believe her ears! She actually felt validated! She hugged her father tightly and practically skipped the rest of the way home.

Another day, Ellen came home with a watercolor she'd painted in art class. She showed it to her mom, who said, "Ellen, this is the most beautiful painting of water lilies I have ever seen!"

Ellen glowed. For the rest of the day, she and her mother laughed, and talked in a way they never had before. That night, the good feeling continued, as Ellen enjoyed the best dinner it seemed she'd ever had, with only her mom and her dad at the table, since Paul was at a friend's house and Gwen was upstairs, asleep. Her mother asked her to show the watercolor to her father. He looked at it in amazement and smiled with admiration.

There was a noise from upstairs then, and her mother went up to see what it was. She came down with Gwen, who was complaining that she woke up due to the racket at the dinner table. When Gwen saw her dad proudly holding Ellen's painting, she grabbed it from him and ripped it in two.

Ellen screamed. Her father pulled as much of the painting back as he could, so Gwen wouldn't tear any more as Gwen cried, "Give me that paper! I want to see it now!"

Ellen's mother took the ripped piece of painting out of Gwen's hand and stuffed it back into her father's open palm, clearly annoyed that once again it was she who had to handle Gwen being upset.

Furious about the damage to her painting, and thinking she would somehow "save the day," Ellen yelled at her mother: "Daddy and I are sick and tired of how you let Gwen ruin everything and never think about us! Right, Dad?"

Her father said nothing. He glanced meekly at his wife, who was trying to coddle blubbering Gwen. In response, his wife gave him a look that could kill.

"I don't know what she's talking about!" he pleaded.

Ellen felt betrayed. Swiping up what was left of her painting, she ran up to her room, crying. Finally she had been acknowledged by both her mom and dad at the same time for having done something right in her life—a beautiful painting. However, even that didn't seem to be good enough to make her parents happy for long. In fact, what seemed like the beginning of a wonderful night, actually turned into a nightmare. Ellen was convinced now more than ever that she could never do anything well enough to get their love.

Meanwhile, downstairs, her parents screamed and yelled, arguing more vehemently than she could recall they ever had before, even though, just a few minutes ago, Mom's attention had been on consoling Gwen. Rocking herself back and forth and trying to console herself under the bedcovers, Ellen listened intently to what was going on one story below. After a few minutes, she found herself wiping some of the tears from her face and telling herself that at least she wasn't the only one ignored this time. This time she got to hear Gwen scream for attention without her mother stopping to take care of her needs before anyone else's.

No one bothered to come upstairs to tend to her. But as upset as Ellen was about the whole painting fiasco, she somehow mustered up one small crumb of satisfaction in knowing that Gwen was being ignored as well this time.

Years later Ellen met Bruce, a nice enough fellow, and they were married soon afterward. As much as Ellen liked Bruce, she found him even more attractive after her mother had first met him for dinner and, amazingly, her mother wasn't the star of the show. He hardly gave her the time of day. Bruce rambled on and on about how proud he was of Ellen being valedictorian.

Ellen thought she adored Bruce, and she knew that he loved her. Once the honeymoon was over, however, she began to take him for granted. She picked on him for every little thing, and nothing he did ever seemed good enough. Ellen complained to her colleagues about how tired she was of her marriage. All Bruce ever wanted to do, she said, was eat Chinese food and watch foreign movies.

As time went on, Bruce chided her that she only seemed interested in her work. He complained that she always stayed later than anyone else and did more work than her boss. He told her she had no insight about office politics. Ellen found herself daydreaming about when she was a little girl and went to work with her dad. Even though he didn't pay much attention to her, she'd cherished every moment with him, and had hoped to get more of that when she grew into adulthood.

This desire had translated into disappointing relationships with men. Rather than accepting the love that came easily and naturally, she sought attention from places that would only leave her disappointed, and those who where there for her never seemed to be good enough.

As time went on, Ellen built a case for leaving Bruce. Almost instinctively, as if saving her life, somewhere in her mind she decided she'd better leave Bruce before he left her.

Four years into the marriage, Ellen was solidly entangled in a no-win trap. She was convinced that if she stayed with Bruce she would die of boredom, but if she left him she wasn't sure that she could handle life on her own. The trap, of course, was more about herself than anyone else. No matter what Bruce did or how perfect a husband he was, Ellen would be unhappy.

One night, after hearing Bruce complain, Ellen stormed out of the house and went to live with a friend from her office. She refused to talk to Bruce when he tried to come by and see her. When she decided to go back and see if Bruce would still have her—mainly because she'd grown overwhelmed, scared, and confused—he was already seeing a woman he'd dated in college and was no longer willing to take her back.

Ellen's roommate helped get her into therapy and a woman's support group. Over time, she learned about what it takes to be in a healthy relationship. It had never occurred to Ellen that her inability to love and accept herself was keeping her from feeling she was being loved and accepted. We'll never know if Bruce was truly the "right" man for her, but we do know that Ellen wasn't living her life in such a way that she could be the "right" one for anybody, especially herself.

She began to recognize how her no-win behavior had a great deal to do with unfinished business from her past. She hadn't realized that she had treated her husband in the same way her parents had treated her. Ellen had rejected Bruce's love because it came to her too easily. She'd believed that the only love worth getting was the kind you had to work for.

She hadn't thought of love as a resting place for the soul. Instead, she believed it was nothing more than a few moments of success and happiness, to be followed inevitably by continual disappointment.

When Ellen finally found someone who loved her, she'd come up with reasons why she didn't want him. This was the essence of her no-win trap: She was unable to receive love and acceptance from those who were willing to give it, and instead strove for the love and approval of those who never would.

If you're in a similar no-win trap, the following points and exercises may help you. Keep a journal if you can. It can provide genuine insights when you look back later and see how far you've come.

Eleven Steps to Escape No-Win Trap 1

How to Bring Love and Acceptance into Your Life

1. *Approach all relationships and opportunities with an attitude of grace and appreciation.* Make a point of not taking anyone or anything for granted. Try to be aware of the disapproval or discontent you may be conveying. Consciously work on your attitude toward your relationship. If you haven't actually entered the situation yet, don't even think about getting involved if you can't have a positive attitude. Don't take

someone or something on if your primary reason is to avoid being alone, or simply to prove you can do it. It's destructive to act as if you're better than everyone else. If you really were better, you either wouldn't be in the situation or you wouldn't be putting others down.

Exercise.   Write down the names of three people who are significant in your life, whether at work or at home. Write down several words or phrases that describe how you treat these people, and see if you treat them as others have treated you in the past. Decide if you want to keep treating these individuals this way or not. Consider what's likely to happen if you do. If you don't like the way they're treating you, consider the part you're playing.

2. *Do not demonize family members.*   Try to see them in a positive light, as people who have worthwhile gifts you can appreciate and learn from. Rather than judging and focusing on everything they did wrong, decide what qualities you want to emulate and what you want to let go of. When you view your parents and family members as either all good or all bad, you'll be more inclined to fall into relationships for the wrong reasons—to either please them or get back at them in some childlike way. If you feel a strong negative charge whenever you think of your parents (and such feelings can be understandable), it's likely that you'll put that charge onto someone who cares for you and seems willing to take it.

Exercise.   Write down five positive aspects for each of your parents, even if they include things you learned from them that you don't want to repeat. Recognize that when you continue to make them wrong in your mind, you're judging them. Try, if you can, to put yourself in their shoes for a moment, as hard as that might be. Try to imagine why they might have acted as they did. Rather than judging, discern and learn what you can from the experience.

3. *Do not idealize your parents.* The concept of idealizing someone is not helpful or fair to both them and you. It sets you up to see them as "bigger than life," keeping you stuck in the position of being a little child. The only kind of relationship you can have in that circumstance keeps those you love at arm's length and as distant fantasies. See them only as people. If you can't, you'll never be able to fully accept others who want to care for you. You'll only hold them up to unattainable standards, and no one will ever win.

4. *Do not idealize anyone, including yourself.* We're all just human beings who make mistakes and yet still deserve love. Therefore, it's important to come to terms with accepting yourself as you are. Otherwise, you'll try to be more, or other, than who you really are, which will keep people from ever knowing you. If you go into work and personal relationships giving people unrealistic expectations of you, you're only setting yourself up for failure and disappointment. Besides, others could feel hurt and deceived by you when they find out later in fact you're not as you seemed to be when they first met you.

   Exercise. Take three people you admire and try looking at them through "reality colored" glasses. List three things you admire about them. Then, without being judgmental, consider three qualities you'd prefer they didn't have. Then decide if you can still admire them the way you do now. Do the same with yourself. The secret to enjoying people is not to overlook what you don't like about them, but to choose to love them while knowing full well how imperfect they are. The same is true of yourself.

5. *Understand that the treatment you received from your parents was more about who they were than who you were.* If you strove to please them and never succeeded, most likely it was because they were intimidated by you or had some issues of

their own. As hard to picture and as pathetically sad as it may be, even when a child is little, some parents are still so brittle and confused from how belittled and "small" they felt due to their childhood experiences that they continue to feel small next to their children. Thus, they may not be able to keep their thoughts or behavior in the realm of the responsible "adult," as Eric Berne, author of the book *Games People Play*, would put it. They keep slipping back into the "child" themselves, and if you experienced this, treated you with the same or similar negative treatment they received when they were younger. (In their minds, they probably believe they treated you better than they were. While this may be true, it still wasn't treatment that would be good for you or what you deserved.) They also may have slipped back to becoming the "parent" where they justified admonishing you for some reason, when in reality they were really acting like a child having a tantrum and judgmentally pointing a finger because they were in a position of authority.

Exercise. Try to imagine what problems and insecurities your mother and father may have been dealing with before you came along. Don't give yourself so much "credit" for their behavior. Ignoring or admonishing you was not their only preoccupation in life. They had problems long before you ever got here.

6. *Choose people and activities where you have a 75 percent or greater chance of succeeding.* If you find yourself going only for the long shots, admit that you're arrogant, easily bored, or afraid of success. Move the goal posts closer. You deserve to get it right at least three times out of four.

7. *Receive compliments gracefully.* You may not realize it, but it's disrespectful to minimize or reject the good graces of others. Make a conscious effort to respond positively. Doing so will increase respect and acceptance from others—and for yourself.

8. *Learn the difference between "taking" and "receiving."* If someone wants to help you, do something kind for you, or give you something that is not illicit or illegal, let them. It is receiving when a person offers you something freely and feels good about having done it. It is taking when you feel they would never have offered if you didn't initiate the action yourself.

   Those who have a hard time receiving from others are often those who complain they're never given anything. I once knew a lady who would always give me back any gift I ever gave her. She bragged to her last breath that no one had ever given her anything and therefore she never owed anybody.

   There may be times where you feel you're in a no-win trap when it comes to receiving things from certain people, such as gifts, services, or favors. You might feel that if you take what they offer, there will be uncomfortable strings attached. On the other hand, if you don't take it, you might be anxious that they'll be offended and there will be some negative retaliation. If this is the case, do what feels most comfortable. There will probably be no way to please this person, and the main issue is that whatever you do may lead to irreparable negative repercussions down the road. We constantly have to discern whether a relationship is advantageous or if it's time to let it go altogether.

9. *Lose your fear of rejection.* When you feel yourself wanting to run because a person you like has something negative to tell you, stand still. There's a good chance they're taking that risk because they want to invest in you, to tell you the truth about what they need so they can stay with you and continue growing closer. See the input as a contribution rather than a criticism. You'll never be in the big leagues of love and acceptance if you can't handle corrective input now and then.

10. *Let others know who you really are, and ask them for what you really need.* Don't confuse someone's inability to psychically know what you need with not loving and accepting you. Speak up. Also, don't waste your time or the time of others by asking for small, piddly things that don't really matter, just to test out how much someone will go out of their way for you.

11. *Become the kind of person you want to have in your life.*

NO-WIN TRAP 2

Everyone Gets What They Want, and What You Get Is Second Best

If you're stuck in this no-win trap, you might say or think:

"I don't really want to go out with this guy, but at least I won't be alone."

"How come I never get what I really want?"

"You always pay more attention to your friends than to me."

"Everything always turns out for everyone but me."

"My mother likes my brother more than me."

"I can never do anything right in my father's eyes."

"How come you're always looking at other women when you're out with me?"

"In your list of priorities, I'm always last."

"You listen to your mother more than me."

"Your game is more important than I am."

"You always have time for the kids but never for me."

"How come I only get what's left over?"

Breaking Free of No-Win Trap 2

Constantly comparing yourself to others makes for a lonely and difficult life. Like the curse of Cain in the story of Cain and Abel, believing you're always treated like the second favorite will make you either try harder or give up altogether. It can also set you up to be the family tattletale or the company hatchet man, so you can feel elevated by chopping others down.

In believing there's only a finite amount of love and opportunity to go around, you set yourself up to think that if you win, someone else has to lose. When you see others doing well, you *automatically* take it as a threat. Rather than enjoying the benefits of surrounding yourself with those who are successful, you settle for those who are doing more poorly than you, or you handpick other small-minded individuals who let you pretend you're king or queen of the hill. You might even find you're jealous of those you love, and think you have to compete with them in order for them to love you. This line of thinking is a sure road to ultimate failure, and a wretched way to run your life.

One of the biggest problems with being caught in the "Cain and Abel Trap" is that while you crave love, recognition, and attention, the amount you do get is never enough. You may even end up acting as if you don't want any attention or recognition, pretending you're above it all and criticizing those who aren't.

If you're the kind of person who always feels they're getting the short end of the stick, those who try to work with you or love you will get the idea that no matter how hard they try, their efforts will be for naught. As a result, they may resist growing close for fear of getting burned. Even your children may come to feel they must never outshine you or receive more attention from the other parent or from anyone else than you. When you always feel "less than," no one can win.

Being stuck in a number-two-mode sibling rivalry can make you feel alone and out on a limb. It takes a real effort to recognize that you're actually already fully connected to the universe, simply by the fact of being here. While it would be nice to receive all the love and approval you feel you missed from your family of origin, it's important to realize that even without it, you're still a worthy person, and that there are plenty of people in the world who do want to love you. The trick is, you have to let them.

Evelyn Gets Her Due

When he was twelve, John lost his parents in a car accident. He had to go live with Aunt Evelyn, who doted on her twin boys, Jake and Al, and made John feel like a male version of Cinderella. John did pretty well in school and always showed up his cousins in baseball. While he initially thought this would make his aunt happy, it only served to agitate her and alienate the twins.

Before John came into the picture, Evelyn knew that her sons, Jake and Al, weren't the greatest students in the world, but it never occurred to her how below average they actually were. Rather than being proud of John, she saw his successful behavior in school as a threat. It didn't help that when she was growing up, Evelyn had been gridlocked in a fierce competition with John's father for their mother's approval.

Evelyn seethed as she remembered how her mom always seemed to bat her eyes at John's dad, Milton. She bought him new clothes for school, while Evelyn had to wear her older sister Margaret's hand-me-downs. Now that Evelyn had her brother's only son under her roof, and potentially under her thumb, it was too easy for her to unconsciously "get back" at her brother by taking it out on his son. Besides, she felt he deserved it. Who did he think he was, showing up her boys?

Years went by, and John somehow withstood Evelyn's lambasting. Every now and then he and Uncle Bill would slip away and go fishing, while Evelyn stayed home and enjoyed watching her twins compete for her attention. Evelyn loved it; she'd never had this much attention as a child.

Uncle Bill had a plumbing business. When he discovered that John was as good with his hands as he was with his brain, he began taking him to work with him. They became good friends, and John proved more than helpful on a number of occasions. Uncle Bill was a lot more comfort to John than Evelyn was, and Bill began to feel the same way about John.

Then, when John graduated high school and turned eighteen, Uncle Bill became disabled. Even though Evelyn had put John down whenever she could in the past, she now recognized that the family was in trouble. Bill couldn't work, and she had her hands full taking care of him and her admittedly "good for nothing" boys. So John became someone of value in Evelyn's eyes, and now it only seemed right that John should take over her husband's business. As far as John was concerned, getting her off his back looked like a good proposition.

However, things with Evelyn didn't turn around completely. As John turned the business into a moneymaker, he took on the position of the man of the house. But while he had all the responsibility that went along with that, he didn't get any of the perks. Evelyn would be civil toward him when it came time to bring home the money, but then it was back to the same old critical routine again.

John ran into one of the tellers of the bank after having done some plumbing at her home. They began going out, and later that year they got married. Evelyn didn't approve of the marriage. She knew that the happier John was, the less she'd have him in her clutches.

As the years passed, the business grew, and John's good business sense, along with his instinctive ability to make the best of a bad situation, helped him gain more freedom from his jealous and mean aunt. Because he could accept the care from his wife, and had learned what not to do from his aunt, he didn't fall into the role of the hurt and angry left-out sibling.

How did John do it? What made him able to resist his Aunt Evelyn's twisted projections? How did he avoid becoming an angry and jealous person himself? It's true that, before they died, his parents had treated him well and had helped him to develop a strong sense of his own identity. But given the undeserved, unfair treatment from his aunt, he could have become disenchanted and let his attitude deteriorate. He didn't. What lessons can we learn from John? And how might Evelyn have viewed her life differently, so as to not feel she had to treat John so poorly?

Nine Steps to Escape No-Win Trap 2

How to End the Cain and Abel Double Bind

1. *If someone mistreated you, or is currently treating you poorly, picture that person as the child they once were.* Consider what they went through before they met you, before they ever became adults. Imagine your parents, or whoever has mistreated you, as the children they used to be. It might even be helpful to look at their family photos and pictures of them as children. Recognize that when they mistreat you, they're repeating the unhappy patterns of their childhood. They are, in truth, much smaller than you are. They were even smaller when you were a child and they were the towering adults! As you practice seeing those who torment you as the children they once were, you'll begin to see they mistreated you because they saw you— not them—as having the real power. When you see them in this light, you'll understand how ludicrous it is to want to treat others in the negative way you've been treated or to go on forever hating those who hurt you from the place of their own childhood wounds.

2. *Fill yourself with happiness and pride when those in your life do well.* See it as a good thing for you too. This is a great exercise to engage in for two weeks. It actually brings a positive benefit to you. You'll see how wishing others well invariably rubs off on you. Also, the truth is, you really do want others' lives to go well. After all, if their lives had gone better, they probably wouldn't have treated you so badly.

3. *Make an "appreciation list."* Pick a few people you know and list everything you've ever received from them. If you can't remember anything you liked, what lesson did they teach you

that was in fact a gift? Perhaps you learned to stand up for yourself, or not to take things too personally. When you come to see that every person in your life directly or inadvertently brings you a gift, sometimes disguised as a lesson, you'll be less inclined to be vindictive, and you'll learn to accept the blessings of the universe.

4. *Try being caring to those you've been complaining about.* If there's someone in your life who you feel is not giving you enough, it could be that you're keeping them from giving more by treating them in a way that prohibits them from doing so. Instead of nagging, criticizing, and complaining about them, offer them some patience and your genuine concern. You may find that treating them with a loving heart brings out the love that's been pushed back and withheld. If they continue to mistreat you in some way, and you feel you're in a no-win trap with them no matter what, then perhaps the best way to "be loving here" is to stand back out of the line of fire.

5. *When you feel ignored, criticized, or rejected, realize that the person doing it to you probably had the same thing done to them.* People don't fight and mistreat others because they have differences, but because they feel they were treated differently. They may incorrectly perceive that in some way that's how you're now treating them. When they see you have something they can't have, or are doing something they can't do, they might feel abandoned, diminished, or intimidated. In its own perverse way, it's a compliment in disguise. Try to take it that way. Don't feed your natural negative reaction. Rise above it and try to understand. If necessary, however, make a point of not letting yourself be the continued recipient of their negative shots. Without being rude yourself, cut the conversation short or only respond in one word answers. Do not continue to be available for them to come down on you.

6. *If you've been hurt by others, make a point of not taking that out on anyone else.* That really hurts both you and them.

7. *If you don't feel loved and understood, appreciate the love and understanding you do receive.* Make a conscious note of it. Remember it and cherish it. And be sure to show your appreciation with thanks, returned kindnesses, and love and understanding of your own. This does not mean that you should interpret crumbs as a five-course meal. It just means to receive what you do get will set the tone for receiving more—perhaps somewhere else.

8. *Remember that love is not a zero-sum game.* Just because your mother doted on your brother doesn't mean she didn't love you. And just because your wife loves your son doesn't mean she doesn't love you too. There is not some finite amount of love available to us that requires dividing it up like a pie and trying to make it go around. The amount of love available is limitless. Rather than picturing your parent or someone significant loving another more than you, picture him or her having enough love to love you all. The more you learn to accept what you do receive, the more you'll receive in return. Unfortunately, we can be so immersed in the rivalry for love, we can even think our children rob the love of our spouses. What if the more someone loves your child, the more they can love you too? You can't win in love by competing. Try winning by feeling "a part" rather than "apart." Indulging your feelings of separation only pushes you further away from any possibility of love and happiness.

9. *Remember that your own talents and success can be intimidating to others.* This doesn't mean you should stop. Rather, it just invites you to be conscious of the fact and be gracious about it when you're around others. Perhaps your family couldn't handle your magnificence when you were a child. If you gave your family your very best, and they gave their love and attention to those who accomplished less, it may have been because

they felt "less than you" themselves. This doesn't make them right and you wrong. It just means they were unable to accept their own inferiority. Don't look for praise and approval from small people. They just can't do it. If you truly want more love and acceptance in your life, strive to be with those who are unafraid to appreciate you.

NO-WIN TRAP 3
You Do Everything Yourself and Get Little in Return

In this no-win trap, you might say or think:

"How come I always get stuck doing everything around here?"

"Why am I always the designated driver?"

"Why am I always left holding the bag?"

"How come you never do anything for me?"

"Why doesn't anyone ever listen to me?"

"I always respected my elders. How come no one ever respects me?"

"I can't help giving my children all my money! They're my children!"

"I could never throw my (45-year-old) son out, no matter how much he steals from us and makes our lives miserable. After all, he's my only son!"

Breaking Free of No-Win Trap 3

This no-win trap is a very difficult situation, since you can find yourself constantly feeling stuck, overwhelmed, and frustrated, especially with your intimate partners and children. If you feel you're in this position, you may find yourself berating and belittling your partner and children for their myriad faults, without meaning to. Perhaps you've been trying too hard for too long to keep them out of trouble, and even covered for them when you thought it was necessary. However, while you did this in the hope of helping them snap out of their immaturity and grow up, perhaps the pressure was too hard on you, and their behavior only became worse.

People in No-Win Trap 3 may want to surround themselves with those who help and care for them, but they seem to gravitate toward those who are so dependent they're hardly capable of helping themselves. The one thing they are dependable for, of course, is that they'll always be there. However, they may not be there in the way you want them to be.

This is the "Martyr's Trap"—ensuring that you'll always be alone—at least in terms of feeling burdened with too much responsibility and no one to share it with—and that you'll do everything by yourself whether you're with other people or not. The sad part is, "being in control" is about the best you can ever expect from this situation. Any possibility of harmonious love or acceptance is absolutely out of the question. The ones who are lucky will one day be out of control long enough to become overwhelmed. At that point—if they're willing to admit to their predicament—they may reach out for real help and finally improve their lives.

That's what happened to Mary.

Mary Meets Her Match—One More Time

Mary was one of those people you could always count on. She always had a smile at work, and stayed long hours after the boss went home. Although she'd been asking for an assistant for years, she was always quick to refuse help from a coworker in order to show what an exemplary employee she was. She was the first to listen, and the first shoulder everyone wanted to cry on.

Everybody at work knew she had war stories from her childhood and a worthless husband at home. She was on her third marriage. As so many of us have done, without even realizing it Mary had made all her important relationship decisions on the basis that the new one was at least "better" than the last, but nowhere close to "good for her." The way she liked to tell it, her father was a drug addict, molested her sister, beat her mother almost daily, and used to berate Mary when she didn't do all the laundry six days in a row.

Compared to her father, husband number one was at least a 50 percent improvement, making him a real sweetheart in Mary's eyes. He only beat her once in a while, usually when he was loaded on some drug or alcohol. Husband number two drank all day but didn't beat her up, another great leap forward. But the drinking eventually wore her down, which led her to husband number three. William was almost perfect. The only problem was, he constantly moved from job to job, and he also spent too much time at the racetrack.

Not only did Mary practice the (unconscious) "better than it was before" theory with the men in her life, she applied it to child rearing too. She considered herself a saint in comparison to her father, and never raised a hand to her children. Instead, she drove herself crazy with her two teenage daughters and nearly six-foot-tall teenage son, telling them at least a hundred times a day to clean their rooms or mow the lawn.

In her eyes, of course, she was only doing everything for everyone's own good, and couldn't understand why she was considered overbearing. One thing was for sure, however: Mary loved her children and her children loved her. The bigger problem was that she could never seem to get it "right" with a man.

Mary's marriage with William went on for a couple of years, with increasingly desperate complaints from her and too many visits to the track for him. It never occurred to her that things wouldn't get better. She just figured she was doing her part by letting William know his behavior was not okay with her.

After William lost his fifth job in two years, things started to be missing around the house, like pieces of jewelry and dollar bills from Mary's purse. One night, when everyone else was asleep, her son Mark came downstairs to complain that the most prized coins from his collection were missing. Mark and Mary looked at each other with that old familiar chill they had shared so many times, then went to check out William's car. Inside his glove compartment they found a bunch of pawn tickets, about $5000 worth of gambling stubs from a nearby casino, and a little bag with some white stuff inside.

The same old pang came back to Mary, the one that always leaked through the wall of denial she'd so strenuously built in her head. In that split second she realized one more time how alone and scared she really was. How she'd only been fooling herself, thinking she had a man behind her, a man who could finally help her feel that she wasn't doing it all by herself. She sent Mark off to bed, telling him to say nothing until she figured out what to do.

This time Mary had to admit to herself that she'd gotten in over her head. She knew that to save herself and her family, she would have to find outside help. Taking a frightening leap of faith, she decided to call a counselor in the morning to help her sort everything out.

The next day, she called a therapist and made an appointment for the first available date. That night, she had to work overtime, so she called Mark at home and asked him to get dinner started. Shortly afterward, William came home and began, as usual, to give Mark a hard time. Mark didn't notice the telltale white specks of cocaine that were still clinging to William's mustache. He felt belittled by William, and feeling overwhelmed and pushed too far, he yelled back that everyone knew that William had stolen his coins. Then he told him what he and his mom had found in William's glove compartment.

All of a sudden, 16-year-old Mark and 47-year-old William were out on the front lawn, brawling away. Mary's daughters, screaming and crying, tried to pull them apart. The oldest girl, Marie, finally ran inside and called the police, then called her mom.

About half an hour later, as her car rolled into the driveway, Mary sank down in the front seat, not believing her eyes. A police car and an ambulance were parked in front of the house, and William was being dragged away in handcuffs. Mark, bleeding heavily, with his sister Marie holding his shaking hand, was put into the ambulance and driven away. Mary and her other daughter followed them to the hospital. All the while, Mary prayed out loud that *this time,* if God would make sure Mark would be okay, she'd promise to never again get entangled with another poor choice of a man.

Following that unforgettable day, William went to jail for drug dealing and assaulting a minor. Mark recuperated quite well from a concussion, a cracked rib, and a broken arm. Mary began attending counseling and Alanon once a week, her two girls frequently joining her in the sessions. Mary finally had time to think about her situation. She knew there was no going back to William, and that she had a lot of changing to do before she even considered getting involved with a man again.

Over time, Mary learned to let go more, to overcome her need to feel in control, and to let a sense of love and discernment rule her life. She learned to let into her intimate life only those who would add to the quality of that life, and to distinguish and stay away from those who would inevitably destroy it.

Seven Steps to Escape No-Win Trap 3

How to Cure the "Martyr's Syndrome"

1. *You only repeat and disdain that which you do not grieve and let go.* When you find yourself in constant patterns of upset with others, take it as a sign that you're playing out something hurtful from your childhood. While it's important to understand what that hurt was about, it's even more important not to waste precious time and energy blaming those from your past life and deriding those in your present. Rather than making everyone else wrong, acknowledge your hurt feelings and recognize that you did not then—and do not now—deserve to be mistreated. This also means not mistakenly mistreating others, even with the best of intentions.

   Make an effort to write down what happened to you as a child that upset you. Let yourself *grieve* that it really wasn't okay, and that you deserved better. In grieving, let yourself genuinely feel what it was like not to get what you wanted and needed so much. This will help you realize that you really *do* want and need healthy people around you now.

   Hurtful things that happened to you as a child weren't done because you deserved them; they happened because the adults who should have been responsible had problems of their own *that ended up on you.* When you recognize that you should be treated better than you were as a child, you'll begin to allow good people into your life, rather than those who only *seem* to be good or are obviously not good for you. When you're finally treated well, you'll no longer believe that things are better when you're simply left alone.

2. *When looking to "recruit" people to be in your life, seek those who would be "good" or "best" for you rather than just "better than last time."* Don't get caught in the trap of comparing who is "relatively" better than who. If you do, you may never get close to what you really want. Don't spend time with people if you only see them as "good for now but not for the long run." If you do, you may be inclined to lower your standards and stay longer than you expected, rather than put your energy into seeking good people for you. Similarly, if you know you're in a situation that's not good for you, do the best you can to make things as palatable as possible, while making effective plans to get out or get real help to make real changes all around.

   Examine carefully the part you played in this current situation, so you don't just repeat the same story in a different place. You haven't learned your lessons about yourself if you simply jump "out of the pan and into the fire."

3. *If you claim you're only staying in a bad situation with someone because they won't make it without you, face your own fear of being alone.* Deep down, those who take the martyr stance about their relationships (and about life in general) are often dreadfully afraid of being left all alone. While they may say they want to run off and be alone, they can't do it for long.

   You'll do a great service for yourself and others if you put more effort into being the person you are meant to be, without blaming others for your misery. You'll also save yourself and others a lot of misery when you avoid being in a bad situation with someone at all. Make sure you don't overlook the red flags that often appear when you first meet someone at a job or in a romantic situation.

Be careful not to bond closely with anyone until you've observed their behavior *over time.* For instance:

- When you're dating a guy and he always has a six pack in his car, take that as a sign to *not* get involved.

- When you're dating a woman who constantly reminds you she can get any guy she wants, and she likes to pick fights *when things are going well,* do *not* get involved.

- When you're on an interview and the interviewer treats his office staff rudely while you're there, know that he will eventually treat you the same way. Don't think naively, "Oh, he'll never treat me that way."

4. *Recognize the difference between people who have "needs" and those who are simply "needy."* Learn to gravitate toward those who maturely recognize they have genuine needs, know how to take steps to effectively meet them, and also know when and how to ask others for help. When you gravitate toward those who are merely needy, it's like entering a bottomless pit: No matter what you do for them, it's never enough.

If you don't want the life of a martyr, then don't attract, cultivate, or reward those whom you can never please. It's up to you to let others know what you're willing to do and what you're not. If you continue to do things while you say you're not willing to do them, in essence you're telling everyone you're willing to do them anyway.

5. *Learn to receive!* Practice receiving without complaining. Make sure you're not being needy yourself. You may have such a need to be needed and/or in control that you make sure no one else can ever give to you. That way of operating ensures that you always "have" to do everything yourself. Practice every day for the next three weeks graciously receiving whatever is given to you, and let the other person know how much

you appreciate them. Don't be picky. Learn to be gracious and accepting. This will become easier over time. If you can successfully do something three weeks in a row, you're on your way to doing it for a very long time, one day at a time.

While you're at it, don't force others to take your advice or insist that they do. For the next three weeks, only ask a person one time if they want your help, advice, food, or anything else. Make sure you're not "pathologically generous," where you insist on giving to others and act insulted when they don't accept. It may feel like you're giving, but in fact you're actually rendering them helpless.

6. *Stop doing everything for others and ask for help yourself.* If you find that you're sick and tired of always having to do it all yourself, the odds are high that as a child you had to handle some aspect of adult responsibilities and/or some inappropriate behavior from an adult. From those early childhood experiences, you became convinced that it's not a good idea to trust people to help or to be there for you.

The problem is, you then unconsciously translate that notion into only engaging with people you cannot trust. *You actually find it easier to just "know" you'll never be able to reciprocally lean on anyone.* You pick people to be with who you know will disappoint you. Somehow that seems like less emotional trouble than honestly seeking out a person whom you genuinely believe to be trustworthy over long periods of time. It allows you to avoid giving your all and taking the risk of being hurt later.

Over the next three weeks, nicely ask one person a day to help you with something one time. If the opportunity doesn't come up, or if the person doesn't seem to listen, say nothing. Just let it go. Next time, ask someone else to do it. Learn to only ask those who will actually do what you ask. If there's a person in your life who always does everything all the time, back off from him or her and try asking someone else. That way you'll be less inclined to overwhelm and burnout the few resources you do have. You'll also come to realize that other untapped resources are available to you.

7. *Try not doing something you normally would.* Pick one thing each day for three weeks: something you don't want to do and that's also not really necessary. If you feel guilty about it, just allow yourself to feel guilty. You may find you don't have to do this thing, and the "guilt" will soon wear off.

   Practice the "sit on your hands" method when you're at dinner or at home with yourself or others. When it comes time to clean up, don't. Just sit there and relax and be gracious. See what happens. Perhaps others will take up the task. If they don't, do not direct anyone to do anything. Just sit.

   If you're alone and take time to relax, you may find you're better company when others join you. A gracious life is not about "doing" all the time. Take time to simply "be." If you're always so busy running around for everyone, you end up by yourself because no one can keep up with you. Slow down and "be here now." You may discover that you've only been running from yourself.

6

Dealing with the
No-Win Trap at Work

What do we live for, if not to make the world less difficult for each other?

George Elliot

*W*e're all familiar with the junglelike games, confused expectations, and potential cold wars that await us every day at the office. Corporate policy and new technologies invite us to think that productivity, happy customers, and good employee morale are the priorities of the day, but increasing requests for stress leave, claims for workers' comp, eruptions of violence at the workplace, and the flood of harassment suits tell us something very different is happening. Combined with the glut of forms and protocols, and the fear of layoffs and Chapter 11s, the focus for business seems to have shifted away from the real work to be done.

Wherever there's small-minded thinking, backstabbing competition, low self-esteem, and the certainty that there's never enough, no-win traps are waiting in ambush. Whether you create them or fall into them, or do both, all the necessary elements are readily available in the office environment. All of the scripts for all the roles are already written in stone—long before anyone even interviews for the job. Just as with adult intimate relationships, the role you take has been learned at home: in the crib, in the sandbox, and right there in your family room. While you may receive support and encouragement at home, it's also where you first develop your fears, denials, and habitual misperceptions.

NO-WIN TRAPS AT SCHOOL

Too often our schools only add to the problem. By cultivating mediocrity and an aversion to risk and creativity, they can forestall the development of one's own authenticity. If you want to observe a test-tube version of the no-win trap, go behind the scenes in a teacher's lounge or principal's office of any elementary school. The teachers who dare to stand out and educate students to become their true selves are far and few between. As in most bureaucratic institutions, much lip service is paid to the notion of fostering individual potential, but there's little real support for those who actually succeed.

Truly great teachers learn how to not intimidate principals, to manage impossible students, to engage parents like ambassadors, and to corral funds from assorted departments without actually stealing. Simultaneously, they must play perfect politics, not hoard the copy machine, work nights and weekends, make sure they use their own coffee mug, and, most of all, not one-up the other teachers. When that proves impossible, they must stuff cotton in their ears, cry to their best friends, and ignore the resentment of colleagues and others.

Every teacher you remember who remained an individual, who didn't try to break your unique spirit, deserves your deepest thanks. It's people like them who helped keep alive your truest inner self. Rules are so easy to hide behind. Those who are willing to risk themselves to bring out their students' potential are like jewelers who can see the diamond in the rough and bring out its light to the world.

Great parents and teachers teach their children and students how to cultivate who they really are, while simultaneously helping them navigate the practical, social side of life, its rules and regulations. Both aspects of life are equally necessary for any real success. This conflict between "being yourself" and "conforming to others" is the basis for many a no-win trap. Those who learn how to keep a sense of themselves while acknowledging and using input from others ultimately move to the head of the class and truly succeed in the game of life.

The kids who lose themselves will achieve another kind of success. By the end of third grade, most of those who will eventually "succeed" in the land of the cubicles have already learned to bury their dreams. They learn to play small, hoard their minuscule power, and lay traps for those who are too bold, too naive, or just too stubborn to play along. After becoming acclimated to how the world works at school, and then fitting into a similar system at work, the notion of becoming "your own true self" becomes a nearly impossible endeavor. With the overriding pressures of corporate interests and the need to earn a living, expressing your own authentic and realized self might be more a cause for dismissal than a reason to commend you for a job well done.

This appears to put us in a fundamental double bind before we even get ourselves to work in the morning. If our real mission on this earth is to become our own authentic selves, then for most of us, just trying to make an honest living is in itself a no-win trap.

There are, however, ways to avoid the trap or to find your way out if you're already in one. If you have any desire to get your work done, continue to be paid, get along better with other people, and still be you, read on. This is your chapter.

THE SOURCE OF WORKPLACE DOUBLE BINDS

In truth, we cannot blame "the outside world" for the no-win trap we experience at work. If you dare to be yourself, make mistakes, try to improve things, or consider new ideas, you're likely to be criticized or ostracized for it, but the source of that antagonism comes from within ourselves—it all started at home.

The workplace is generally made up of people like us who grew up within a family, or some similar intimate social grouping. They carry, from the past, beliefs and predispositions, conditioned by the social group they were part of and their interaction with it, the same challenges to holding their own while fitting in with those around them. The family is their first social experience; it shapes the way they see themselves and others. The adjustments they make to family life become habitual elements of their character. In a very real way, we all bring our families into the workplace with us.

Those in the office who are busy trying to slough off, blame others, dominate, overcome, overwhelm, steal recognition, seize authority, placate, insult, pretend, fake, abuse, torment, and demean—all in the name of earning a day's pay—are operating under the influence of their childhood family. If you find you're the corporate scapegoat, fix-it person, office martyr, or donkey that keeps holding out for a carrot, you're also operating "under the influence." Trying too hard, being too agreeable, picking fights at the wrong time, having a really good idea, standing alone, making dumb mistakes in front of the wrong people, being too self absorbed, or daring to dream—all of these can bring out conflicts that lead to a no-win trap.

What you may not realize is that as you fall into this no-win trap of insults and rejection, you could simultaneously be setting no-win traps for the very people entrapping you! While you're feeling powerless and licking your wounds, certain that the entire office is out to get you, those who have trapped you could actually be feeling the same way about you! Both parties can feel intimidated, shown up, put down, disrespected, or unable to make the money they feel they deserve. It's only through the diligent practice of self-awareness that you can begin to see the true nature of this give and take in no-win traps.

Bottom line: Where there is childish behavior among adults, left-over grievances from childhood are involved. We need to examine the part we play in creating these no-win traps, gain insight into how to step out of them, and hopefully generate a new, more peaceful way to earn our daily bread. Perhaps then we can make the world less difficult for each other.

Signs of a Childhood-Based No-Win Trap at Work

There's one sign that stands out in particular, and it can be summed up in one word: small.

There's nothing worse than the sting of small-time backbiting between those who call themselves adults but act like sniveling children. In between making real estate deals, playing to the jury, performing surgery, listening to suicidal patients, or dispatching major fires, the thing that breaks our spirits are those breakroom rumors, raised eyebrows, or nasty e-mails that make us somehow feel slighted and small.

While it may appear that "small" things, like letting your office manager know you read his memo or restocking the toilet paper in the rest room, don't need to be taken seriously, in reality, they do. The word *small* here doesn't refer to making a mountain out of a mole-hill—although a no-win trap can be made of that—but to those seemingly minor gestures that invite someone to feel small, to be made to feel unimportant and unworthy of respect.

Consider this for a case in point: The next time you're at a gas station and you dare to use the rest room, notice how grateful you are if you can actually take a full breath in there or if there's an actual sheet of toilet paper left on the roll. If the rest room is clean and well-stocked, you'll be more inclined to go back to that station for gas. If not, you could feel so belittled you'll never go back there for gas again.

It's the same way at work. How often do you have the experience of feeling "big" at the job? How often do you feel "small"? How much do you contribute to others? Do you add or do you take away? Are you often misunderstood? How did that come to be?

If you're perceived to be the "culprit" who somehow ignores, slights, or makes someone feel small, it's likely that they'll retaliate in some way, with some petty remark or gesture of their own. And yes, you could then feel the exact same way, and want to "dis" them in return. Soon you've got a minor feud going on, with each of you dissing the other.

How do these small issues get so big? Why do we act so small?

The following stories and insights might help you to be more aware of the vestiges of sandbox behavior that hinder you from becoming the balanced, mature, and satisfied person you want to be.

NO-WIN TRAP I AT WORK

Feeling Your Work Is Never Good Enough, but You're Too Good for Your Job

You may have issues with all three of the basic no-win traps, or perhaps this is the one you're most prone to fall into. Look at the following lines and phrases and see which ones relate to you. If what you read sounds terribly familiar, then No-Win Trap 1 may be your biggest problem at work. The good news is that with awareness comes the possibility of healing, and with healing, self-empowerment is only a matter of time and disciplined determination. Those stuck in this no-win trap may find themselves saying:

"I never feel good enough at work."

"I'm always afraid to ask for time off."

"If I let anyone know that I need help, they'll take away my promotion."

"The boss doesn't like me."

"I've got to save this department. That will certainly help my career."

"I was only trying to help. Why is everyone so mad?"

"I just landed the biggest contract this company has ever seen and all they can do is complain about how I used somebody's coffee mug by mistake."

"I don't care how hard my boss makes my job, I'll just work as hard and as long as I have to and I'll show him up in due time."

"How come everyone admits I'm the smartest architect they have here, but when I stand up to the boss in a design meeting, no one stands up for me?"

"I just can't understand why things only got worse when I sent a letter of complaint to my boss's boss. After all, he was treating me badly and I do have my rights, don't I?"

"I don't care how many people don't like you as a boss. I'll always be there for you. You can count on me."

Breaking Free of No-Win Trap I

There are many ways this trap can show up at work. Some of them may surprise you. You may unknowingly give the impression that you think you're better than everyone else, when deep down you wonder if you are even good enough to do your job. Without realizing it, you may be overcompensating, trying so hard that others who are only "doing what was asked of them" believe you want to show them up. They may never know that in fact what you want is the acknowledgment and recognition you never got at home.

Consider the following case concerning a woman who comes to make peace with what she could realistically expect in return for doing a good day's work.

Renee's Path Out of Her No-Win Trap

Renee is someone who successfully found a way out of her self-made double bind. She had undergone severe physical and mental abuse in her childhood, but hadn't begun to recognize the impact of this abuse until she engaged in psychotherapy as an adult.

Renee had a childhood that by most people's standards would have been considered extremely difficult. Yet, as with many of us, at the time, her feelings about it were ambivalent: Sometimes it seemed tolerable to her, other times impossible.

She was the eldest of two children. Her father was like a spoiled child, a needy alcoholic who saw people in the family as objects to meet his needs. He mainly expressed anger, and would beat Renee's mother, especially when he was drunk.

Renee felt that her mother cared for her as best she could. She seemed to have spent most of her time at work, cleaning houses and cooking at a nearby restaurant. These were the only jobs her husband would let her do, and she went willingly, mainly to get away from him, and to bring home enough money to stave off his anger for a while. She always felt bad leaving Renee at home with her father, but it seemed to her that she had little choice in the matter.

By the time Renee was 7 years old, she'd learned ways to win her mother's love and support—at least when her mother was available. She had also come to realize that her father didn't care who got the brunt of his anger. He directed physical blows and verbal tirades to any family member who happened to be nearby when he flew into a rage.

It was at this tender age of 7, and probably earlier than that, that Renee enrolled herself in the family drama, as the dysfunctional scapegoat, the hero child with the compulsive need to save the under-dog. Unfortunately, more often than not, Renee found herself as the underdog everyone else stepped on. However, she seemed not to mind taking on that potentially dangerous position. Her great purpose in life was to rescue her mother from her father's abuse. This, she believed, would help her mom retain enough energy to work more and make more money, and, more important to Renee, to focus her energy in a positive way in her—Renee's—direction. Although it was complicated, Renee's efforts sometimes actually succeeded.

Children learn to pick up crumbs of love and attention by what-ever means possible. Unfortunately, they may continue in this pattern for the rest of their lives. From an early age, Renee came to believe that in order to enjoy the pleasure of love and success, she had to willingly take abuse from others, play the scapegoat, and be the one who was blamed for everything. Even to this day she finds herself saying, "It wasn't all that bad," when in fact it is truly amazing how much she went through while still managing to retain her sanity.

At the age of 37, Renee found herself beginning her second mar-riage while having grave difficulties at work and in her personal life. She was afraid the marriage would wind up in divorce. And having thrown everything she had into her jobs, she'd never had children, and so never received the love and comfort of having a family of her own—the very thing she missed most in life.

After a couple of therapy sessions, it became evident that as a child Renee had been involved in a number of complicated no-win traps. Still, she was initially unaware of how complex these situations were. Gradually, as her scapegoat role and her need to save the day as a wannabe hero came to light, she began to make headway.

In sessions, Renee talked a great deal about the temporary man-agement job she had at the bank, filling in while the regular manager, Christine, was out on surgical leave. Renee was excited about the chal-lenge of this new position. She was also zealously fulfilling her old wannabe-scapegoat-hero role, and saw the job as an opportunity to prove herself and truly become "one of the fold." She was not aware, however, of the dangers in trying too hard in a politically delicate work environment.

During the four months that she served as temporary manager, teller morale went up, positive customer feedback skyrocketed, and no customer ever had to wait in line more than five minutes.

Renee was incredibly proud of herself. She was elated whenever one of the employees stated how glad she was to have her at the helm. But somewhere in the excitement, everyone seemed to forget that Christine would be coming back. Well, not everyone had forgotten.

The vice president at the main bank, the man to whom Renee reported daily by phone, seemed only mildly pleased with her accomplishments. From the tone of his voice, Renee sensed that he was neither as appreciative nor as positive as she wanted him to be. In fact, the more significant the improvements our heroine made, the less enthusiastic he became.

Then, shortly before Christine was scheduled to return to work, the vice president paid Renee a visit. Almost as soon as he opened his mouth, Renee's stomach began to churn with anxiety and her heart sank with the foreboding old feelings of pending doom. Just when she thought she'd done all that had been requested of her, the vice president explained in his monotone that she had "shown up" Christine.

"We're not sure just where to place you when Christine comes back," he said. "We don't want the employees at your branch looking to you instead of Christine for answers. That would cause a rift among the staff." A few days later, Renee was made supervisor of the drive-through window. Though a staff member in Human Resources explained that it was a lateral move from her old position, it felt like a slap in the face to her. She was also told she should not have expected any long-term gains from her temporary assignment. Of course, it would be noted in her employee file that she'd done a good job as temporary manager.

With no more than a curt smile from Christine and whispered promises of loyalty from other tellers, Renee assumed her new position at the drive-through window. As customers continued to ask for Renee, Christine complained about the unauthorized changes that had been made in her absence. Renee realized that she needed to get back into Christine's good graces, but she had no idea how. She felt utterly helpless and seemed unable to improve the situation.

She was once again in a no-win trap. If Renee went along with Christine's way of doing things, she was afraid of appearing to abandon those customers and coworkers she had promised to support. On the other hand, if Renee continued doing the special services for customers and favors for employees that had made her so popular over the past few months, she was sure Christine would write her up and ultimately dismiss her from her job. Renee's zeal to save the day and carve a niche of recognition for herself blinded her to the role she actually played in the overall picture.

It was at this point that Renee decided to enter therapy. She was determined to find a way to get through without losing or once again paying too high a price.

With the increasing objectivity she developed in her therapy, Renee began to see that the harder she tried to please Christine, the more she was being mistreated. She began to understand her pattern of looking for positive reinforcement from people who were disinclined to give it. It was something she'd done all her life—made herself vulnerable to people who were not on her side. The vice president at the bank, for instance, didn't care about her excellent performance; he saw her role as simply filling in and keeping a low profile, not shining like a star.

Eventually Renee found another job. And this time she made a point of not looking to her supervisor for too many strokes. As time went on, she thrived at this new job. She no longer overcompensated by outdoing others and trying to prove herself. Instead she put out the energy required without over- or underdoing things. This pleased her supervisors. She'd learned that the workplace, like life, has many mixed messages and unfair aspects, and she did not have to be the one to fix them all. Renee found life at work was smoother and more successful when she calmly went with the flow of events and organizational changes, without trying too hard.

Recently, Renee received a promotion. She now feels that her life doesn't depend on her proving herself. All she needs to do is to be competent in her work—not try to outshine everyone else.

Consider the following tips to help you steer as clear as possible from any no-win traps that could come your way.

Nine Tips for No-Win Trap I

How to Escape Being the "I'm Not Good Enough" Employee

1. *Ask for what you need.* Don't give the impression that you'll put up with anything, and don't act as if you don't need anything from others. Consider what you essentially need and make a request for it—without long explanations or putting your tail between your legs. If everyone else gets a vacation, and it's important that they do, recognize that you deserve it also. Ask for what you want and simply wait for the answer. If you don't get the dates you prefer, have an alternative prepared. From here on in, act as if you deserve what everyone else deserves, and don't be apologetic about it. Over time, you'll get used to receiving what is already yours.

2. *Get help when you need it.* Instead of being afraid of looking incompetent if you need to ask for help at work, recognize that part of the responsibility of having your job includes knowing what you can do yourself and when you need the help and input of others. Whether you're the project manager for a major exploration into outer space or you work in a distribution plant for domestic cars, you'll never rise to the top if you can't let the right people know at the right time when your project needs help. In fact, the sooner you ask for help *from those who are actually able to help you,* the more respected you will be. Trying to save the day by yourself is the most direct and immediate route to disaster.

3. *Focus on your own behavior, not that of your boss.* Rather than taking your boss's apparent dislike for you as a personal issue, consider for a moment what you may do that makes his job difficult for him. All too often basic logistics and simple situational double binds turn into interpersonal double binds because everyone feels the other party is personally out to get them. Before going down that road, consider first the possibility either that you don't take another person and their job seriously or that you deter their ability to be effective in some

way. Rather than seeing your relationship with your boss as an isolated event, consider what might be going through his or her head over time:

Is it possible that your behavior puts your boss in a difficult situation in some way? For instance, do you come in late? Do you do good work some days and slack off on others? Expect special treatment for performing extraordinarily well? Demand more attention than others? Drain him or her in some way? Is it possible, without realizing it, that you invite your boss to feel that he or she has no control over you or isn't able to do his or her job?

4. *Don't try to be the one to save the day.* Never go out on a dangerous limb in hopes of saving the day unless you're the CEO and you are being paid to do such a thing. If you find yourself lying in wait for some "Mighty Mouse" way to creatively save your department from utter doom, sit back and contemplate the situation. Even Mighty Mouse follows the motto, "Fools go where angels dare not tread." Saving the day in a corporation requires a team effort directed by those in authority from up above.

Also, if you believe that pointing out the flaws in upper management is a way of single-handedly saving the day, guess again. Simply do the best you can within the realm of the position that's given to you. Inching out into a new territory that's not supported by those above you is a surefire route to disaster. If you have to save the day, become an entrepreneur and start your own company, one financed by money generated by you alone. When you're truly footing your own bill from the ground up, you'll have plenty of chances to save the day—all the time.

5. *Do not confuse accomplishment with entitlement.* Recognize the importance of both respecting others' possessions and boundaries and doing a good job. Don't think that because you just completed a difficult assignment, you have the right

to walk into your boss's office, sit down, put your feet on his desk, and relax. Often, those who don't feel good about themselves come from households where their personal boundaries were not acknowledged. This could carry over to your workplace, where you either act like you don't mind not being respected within your own boundaries or you may not be considerate of the boundaries of others.

After having enjoyed bringing in an especially good sale, or writing a grant that brings in a great deal of money, you might feel you have the right to be casual and familiar with those bosses and coworkers. That may not be the case. It also doesn't make it okay to take one of the cigars off your boss's desk without him offering it to you, or thinking you can simply join the partners on their boat for lunch without having been invited. You still need to wash your own coffee cup and make sure you close the fridge in the employee lounge.

6. *Praise in public, and discuss your needs or differences in private.* No matter how correct you think you are, never use meetings of any sort to stand out, gloat, contradict someone, or belittle anyone in the room. In fact, never criticize anyone if you disagree. Instead, ask them to help you with their line of thinking so you can to gain insight into their point of view. Try it. Everyone else might like it, and they may treat you better too.

7. *Don't go over your boss's head.* Few disasters have as far reaching repercussions as going over your boss for any reason. In fact, the only time to ever speak to your boss's boss is to let him or her know how wonderful the company is and how well everything is going. Don't expect your boss's boss will treat you better than your boss does.

If you feel you're being mistreated and need support on how to cope with the situation, consider all the angles of politics within your corporation first. Speak to a safe mentor—outside the company, if possible—and get some professional help, as necessary. If you need to see an attorney or to seek medical help, certainly do so. Be careful, however, about pointing fingers and making others wrong. The backlash and anger may put you in an extremely difficult position. When you go for help and input, make sure your words are truly held in confidence, and carefully consider all your options. You may find a way to improve your situation by moving to another department, or by altering your stance or behavior in some way. While you always do have the option of going over your boss's head, make sure that action doesn't set you up to fall deeper into the trap you're already in. Only seek help from safe places.

8. *Appreciate others, and you will be appreciated.* Consider the possibility that if you don't feel acknowledged by your boss, there's a chance he or she doesn't feel respected or acknowledged by you. Without meaning to, you could be giving the impression that "as soon as my big deal comes through, I'm blowing this pop stand." Rather than acting as if you're too good for your job or the company in general, try cultivating an attitude of appreciation that, at least for the present, you're glad to have this job. If you need to seek other places of employment, do so, but in a low profile way. And remember to consider who your three recommendations will be. Instead of burning bridges, consider those who may be helpful to you, and do what you can to make their lives easier without jeopardizing yours.

   In the case where you don't respect your boss, at least respect the position. If you can't do that, perhaps deep down you don't even respect yourself.

9. *Don't allow yourself to be taken advantage of.* Be careful not to be used by others who pick up on your need to be accepted. Instead of burning out by giving 200 percent of yourself on the job, begin with giving them 75 percent and go from there. (It's likely your 75 percent is most people's 100 percent.)

   This is a common no-win trap for those recent and enthusiastic advanced degree and law student grads who are just dying to prove themselves or try out their new corporate management or urban planning skills. As much as you may know concerning book knowledge, you're still green around the corporate political gills. Be careful. You may be in over your head when up against the challenge of a businessperson who picked him- or herself up by their own boot straps years ago and has been playing people against each other ever since.

Consider the notion that a boss who may or may not be well liked needs to have someone play hatchet man, or to bring new directives from up above to resentful employees in his department. It could be about budget cuts, or new protocols for paperwork—any changes can rile the troops. If you're cited for doing good work and are known for being loyal at all costs, your boss could ask you to do all kinds of unsavory things, rewarding you with pats on the back and occasional perks that invite you to feel special and acknowledged.

Make sure that what you're doing is openly sanctioned by the company as well as by the law. When it comes time to say who's accountable for your actions, be careful you're not caught out on a limb by yourself. Being a company henchman has few perks, a high price, and is usually short-lived.

While it's a jungle out there, someone has to win, and it might as well be you. In fact, the real source of empowerment is a safe and effective space within your work environment, which you could create not only for you, but for as many others as possible.

NO-WIN TRAP 2 AT WORK

Feeling "Everyone Gets but Me, and What I Get Isn't Good Enough"

Without even realizing it, every day at work you could be playing right into the old story of Cain and Abel, due to some leftover sibling rivalry issue you may not have even known you had. The way this particular childhood-based no-win trap plays out in adulthood can be subtle and insidious. Because you didn't get what you wanted or needed as a child, by the time you're an adult you might be so used to being beaten down that you're not even consciously aware of how long you've gone without. Or you might be at the other end of the spectrum, continuously whining to your coworkers about how you never get what you want—until they begin to ignore you completely.

If you're wondering whether this trap is a concern for you at work, consider the following statements and see if any of them ring a bell:

"Everyone gets away with murder around here except for me."

"How come the harder I work, the more the boss likes Bill? His work doesn't hold a candle to mine."

"The only way to get respect around here is to let them think I'm mean."

"I've worked so hard around here to carve out my niche, I'll be damned if anyone is going to take it away from me!"

"I'm sick and tired of how John always gets his way and I'm the one to always give in."

"Just wait till I'm the boss around here, I'll get back at all of them. I'll treat people just like they treated me, and they'll get a taste of what it's like."

"I am so angry about having been totally ignored in my family. I'll never take that from anyone again! If a boss or coworker has the nerve to look past me like I'm not there, they'll be sorry they ever came to work!"

"How come I always mind my own business, but no one ever gives me credit for being a good employee?"

"Why is it that anything that goes wrong around here is always my fault?"

"I don't really like reporting people to the boss, but it sure gets me a lot of attention from her. Besides, they deserve it. I do so much that no one gives me credit for."

Breaking Free of No-Win Trap 2

While it may be difficult to admit you relate to the above statements, this is a good time to consider whether any of them apply to you. Even if you don't have feelings of the sort expressed, you could possibly fall prey to those who do. Give yourself a lot of credit. If you grew up in a family where you had brothers and sisters, you no doubt had some tactics that aided in your survival. If you were an only child, you certainly developed skills that manipulated both Mom and Dad.

Sibling rivalry is a feeling in your gut that can surface like an angry dragon when you least expect it. When it gets the best of you, you can feel competition with just about anyone and anything at any time. Sibling rivalry is not just about whether you're jealous of your brothers or sisters. In fact, in the big picture, it's not about them at all. They're only living symptoms in your mind, persistent feelings that you're second best, that you always give and never get.

The issue of sibling rivalry relates to your doubts about yourself, about whether you'll have your needs met, and whether you'll be accepted for who you are. Your perceptions of your brothers and sisters, and of how you think your parents feel about all of you, are only a kind of rationale to explain what you believe about yourself. You could be the favorite child in the family, and think that what you get is still not good enough. You could be the last one on the family list, and still be happy to know you're loved. Believe it or not, the choice is yours.

Contrary to the popular cliché, the world is not divided between the "haves" and "have-nots"; it's divided between those who believe they will ultimately have their needs met and those who believe they won't. It's important to recognize which of these ideas you carry in your head.

At home, you could be jealous that your spouse pets your dog more than she hugs you. You could find yourself competing with your new beau's teenagers, just when you thought things were going well. If you're experiencing this competition at home, you could suddenly find yourself arguing with someone in the lunchroom, just because they took your usual parking spot or borrowed your phone book and forgot to ask first. When you're stuck in the Cain –and Abel Trap at work, you'd rather die than give another person the benefit of the doubt. You may even feel you already have, but the bottom line is, you're suffering from believing everyone gets but you.

At work, it might be that just when you thought you'd be reward-ed for offering to cut down on your hours when no one else did, you're asked to leave because it appears you don't really need the job! Or you may have enjoyed being the highest ranked salesperson in the show-room for the past ten years when, all of a sudden, some new person comes in and tells you the boss wants them to use your office. You might take that to mean you've just lost your hard-won prestige. On the other hand, it could very well mean that you just got a promotion. At the very least, you might be able to make the change work to your advantage in some way.

Any way you look at it, be proud of yourself for having gotten this far in life. But also take into consideration whether you want to alter any of the ways you handle situations, or the tools you've used to get you where you are. While it's ever so important not to allow your-self to live and work in fear, it does us no good to deny the growing increase in stress and pressure in our lives at home and in the office.

In fact, we live in a time when, more than ever, it's important to recognize how much each of us really does count. No matter how unimportant we might feel we are, based on how our families treated us when we were young, or how uninfluential we may feel we are to the big world out there, a single word or gesture we use while driving, socializing, giving promotions, laying people off, or waiting in line for a restroom could have serious consequences, and in some cases might mean the difference between life and death.

Before going into a tirade because you thought someone dis-counted you in some way, consider the notion that perhaps you didn't have all the information. Always be willing to listen to others before jumping in with your own demands.

If you're proud that you're finally becoming a genuine entrepre-neur, make sure you're committed to being a mature adult employer, rather than an overgrown child who finally has the reins and wants others to suffer as you have in the past. At the risk of sounding macabre, I believe you should never underestimate the potential effects of the growing number of weapons people carry in their cars, or even when going to work. Also, consider the amount of damage they can do if in order to work for you, they need to carry a set of keys to your home.

What used to be relatively minor skirmishes often develop now into major problems, landing in courtrooms and emergency rooms. The main precaution one can take is to make the commitment to employ within yourself the discipline, insight, leadership, and maturity that will work positively for you and those around you. The misuse of newfound power to make up for the past only keeps you firmly implanted in your old, childhood no-win traps.

If a person feels they were treated worse than others at home as a child, they can carry that hurt with them for the rest of their lives in a way that affects everything they do. In your dealings with such people, you can never be certain how an offhand remark or gesture might be taken. The way you treat them could come back to haunt or hurt you, even though your actions might be thoroughly justified. You never know how much pain a person may have been harboring all these years, and how close to the edge he or she feels, especially when overwhelmed by multiple stresses.

The following case shows how close to the surface someone's hidden hurt and anger can be, without that person, or anyone else around him, having any idea about it.

Silent Sam Sees the Light

Sam was a bookkeeper for a large manufacturing company. His boss, Herbert, was a ruthless tyrant despised by the men and women he supervised. Most of the staff talked about Herbert behind his back. Expressing anger directly to him would have been cause for immediate dismissal.

Everyone knew what a terrible guy Herbert seemed to be, but they had no idea how poorly he'd been treated by his family when he was growing up. As an adult, he was merely following in the footsteps of his volatile and out-of-control father, who had beaten him as a child on a daily basis. While those experiences obviously did not make his behavior at work acceptable, they did make Herbert feel justified to act the way he did, and the company found good use for his talents, promoting him to the unsavory position of hatchet man.

Herbert had no problem laying off large groups of people at a time, and he had an unrivaled system for managing the books. His boss knew just how to make him feel important, and found it easier and easier to look the other way when Herbert did his dirty work. Compared to how much Herbert had felt terrified and alone in his family, playing the part of henchman to his boss and getting a hefty enough bonus check every Christmas to stave off his henpecking wife was as close to heaven as he was ever going to get.

All the while that Herbert was managing his department like a medieval serfdom, Sam didn't complain to anyone about him. Sam was seen as the nice guy who did his job competently and seemed unaffected by his oppressive boss. He was also apparently unaffected by the negative comments of other employees. When Herbert blew up and yelled at people, including Sam, Herbert's wrath seemed to just roll off him. In fact, Sam had no conscious notion that Herbert affected him at all.

Sam had grown up in a family of four brothers and sisters where it was assumed that he would be the brunt of jokes, torment, and ridicule. His older brother was the family favorite, his two sisters were basically ignored, and Sam came to the conclusion early on that the only attention he would ever get was derogatory comments from his siblings and his parents. Since he was generally a loner, Sam basically grew up and went about life not giving human inequities much thought. He went about his own business, outwardly accepting everything; it was pretty much as things had always gone for him in the past. Until one day.

The only books Sam ever liked to read were murder mysteries and science fiction. One spring Saturday afternoon, however, as he was perusing new releases at a major bookstore chain, he overheard an author who was speaking at her book signing and decided to take a seat, which was thoroughly out of character for him.

Sam listened as she and the audience interacted over issues concerning self-esteem and workplace environments. While the words seemed to go in one ear and out the other, Sam noticed an attractive woman who was sitting nearby. She was actively asking questions and appeared to be enjoying herself.

Afterward, Sam engaged in his second uncharacteristic behavior for the day, and he wound up ordering some exotic cappuccino blend at the store's coffee bar. As if he were in a trance, he shuffled his way to a group of people who had been to the book signing and sat down. He found himself enthralled as he listened to the discussion, largely led by the woman who had asked so many questions at the signing a few minutes before.

It wasn't so much that he cared about the issues raised in the discussion, although the words struck a remotely hidden internal chord; it was just that he felt so included in this ad hoc group of strangers, perhaps for the first time in his life. He basked in the atmosphere, barely noticing that he drank the exotic coffee blend he'd ordered. Then, to his surprise, he began to want to engage in the ongoing discussion. Valiantly mustering the courage to speak, he was just about to ask the pretty woman a question, when . . .

Of all people, Herbert, his boss, walked in with his wife. She was berating him, as usual, saying something about how he never pulled out his wallet fast enough when it came time to pay. Just as Herbert was taking this embarrassing rebuke from his spouse, he turned to the comfortable seating arrangement in the coffee bar and couldn't believe his eyes.

Right there in front of him was his very own serflike employee, Silent Sam, the one who never stood up for himself, never rocked the boat, and always took whatever he dished out. Herbert focused eyes on Sam, and Sam and his group looked up and noticed Herbert.

Sam's eyes bulged, and in seconds, venom welled up within him. Unable to contain all his pent-up frustrations—feelings that had been swirling inside him for 42 years—Sam stood up and shook his finger at Herbert as if he were Exhibit A in a courtroom and his new friends were the jury. From deep inside, some forgotten sense of worthiness and acknowledgment appeared, and Sam felt spontaneously safe and supported enough to come forward and reveal just how horrible it was to suffer the mistreatment that Herbert inflicted. He went on to say that he would never subject himself to such indignity ever again. Sam let Herbert have it so thoroughly, the entire room stood up and cheered, to the point of practically starting a riot.

Then there was silence. Herbert looked at Sam and, for once, realized he had nothing to say, mainly because he feared for his survival. His wife looked at Sam, the crowd, and Herbert, and dragged him out of the coffee bar the way a mother would her naughty little boy.

Sam sat down in a stupor, and everyone came over to congratulate him for standing up to his boss. His usual quiet self now, he looked to the woman next to him, and said, "Now what do I do?" She smiled and handed Sam her card. It said she was an attorney who specialized in employee rights at the workplace. Sam thanked her profusely and took a long walk home. Although he knew he was probably out of a job, for the first time in his life he felt like a man, like someone with a voice who had finally been heard. And besides . . . he noticed in the handout he'd picked up in the bookstore that on Sunday they were having a book signing and workshop with the author of a book about redoing your résumé and starting a whole new career!

As much fun as the ending was in Sam's particular case, today's reality often involves much sadder endings. We've all seen the headlines of office shootings and other violent eruptions at the workplace, and we should all try to be aware of what might be lingering under the surface. If you or someone you know is feeling hurt or overwhelmed by those who delight in making others feel small, or if you find yourself feeling or acting hostile to others, whether at home, the workplace, or out in the world at large, please give the following points serious consideration.

Ten Tips for No-Win Trap 2

Don't Be the "Everyone Gets but Me" Employee

1. *Avoid the "small" traps.* Be aware of when someone is inviting you to feel small at work, and get in touch with your feelings

about it. Rather than letting them think it's okay with you, be more formal with them in your interactions for a while, so they recognize that you were offended. Don't fall into the trap of getting mad and complaining about their behavior. Simply make yourself less available for the smallness and petty inflictions of others. Do not let your good nature be misinterpreted to mean you're someone who thinks that anything goes.

2. *People don't care how much you know until they know how much you care.* When training or critiquing someone at work, take this old adage into account. If you need to critique a coworker's work or behavior, do it in such a way that they recognize you care. When you point out to him or her that they're doing something wrong, take care to ensure that they don't misunderstand and think you disrespect them as a person. No one can take information well when they feel you're making them small or insignificant. In fact, the smaller you invite someone else to feel, the more they'll be inclined to get back at you sometime later.

3. *When it comes to jokes, if in doubt, don't.* For those of you who tell jokes when you're trying to lower the tension in the room, make others feel comfortable, or make yourself feel better in some way, think ahead about whether it will make someone else feel small. Also, be certain you're not joking in retaliation for someone making you feel less than wonderful. Be the bigger person and end it here.

4. *Always recognize the input of others.* Make a point of acknowledging anyone's input at any time as a contribution of some sort. If someone brings you a thought that you may not see as helpful, simply thank him or her for their input and leave it be. Be aware that it's human nature for someone to confuse a rejection of an idea with having been "put down." Never criticize anyone to make yourself feel better. Rather than making them wrong, politely acknowledge their effort: "Thanks for your input. I'm glad you told me."

5. *Don't be the office martyr.* Do not volunteer to take the worst piece of equipment in the office or the chair with the broken leg. If others see that you're willing to take second best, they'll treat you that way. In case you've already fallen into that pattern, without making a big to-do, next time get in line sooner for a new piece of equipment, or perhaps bring a new plant into your office to show you have self-worth.

6. *Reexamine your office relationships.* Consider everyone you work with and the relationship you have with him or her. If it's possible that you invite them to feel small in some way, make a point of acknowledging how much you appreciate them—without being condescending or patronizing.

7. *Don't join "cliques."* Recognize the danger in being cliquey at work. It backfired in junior high, and it won't do much more for you now. The old adage, "You have to be little to belittle," is true today. It's amazing how we all still need to feel that we're special, and at the same time that we also belong. Do not pursue these feelings at the expense of other people; it's only a sign of how little you think of yourself. Make a point of inviting the new employee to have lunch with you, and treat others the way you'd like to be treated. If you need a pragmatic reason, consider the notion that you never know when you'll need this person, and there could be a day when they supervise you.

8. *Think about everyone you work with: If murder were legal, would you still be here?* A word to the wise is sufficient.

9. *Beware of your own hidden anger.* If you're constantly feeling hurt, consider that you may be angry without realizing it. It never hurts to get some counseling or sign up for an anger management class. You may be closer to the edge than you realize. We could all use this advice at one time or another. Those who tend to need it the most are the ones most unwilling to go. Don't keep yourself from help simply to protect your ego.

10. *Don't ignore your feelings.* If you act as if you don't mind how everyone is treating you, you're likely to blow up sometime later in a kind of "delayed response." Try to be in touch with how you really feel, and don't allow yourself to be the brunt of others' jokes. You'll be less inclined to let it build up inside and lose control later on. The first time someone says something you don't appreciate, let them know you want to be available to do a good job for or with them, but their comment made it that much harder. The difficulty is, you may not know how hurt you are until after the fact. If that's the case, be more distant for a while, until they get the hint to back off.

In the meantime, talk about your feelings in a safe place so you can get the hurt off your chest and not harbor it until it erupts later. Part of knowing you aren't second best is allowing yourself to be in touch with your feelings. If you don't think your feelings count, no one else will either. If you hurt at the pit of your stomach, know that everything isn't okay. Write a letter about how you feel and read it to someone you trust before you decide what to do next. Do not send or e-mail hurt feelings to a person or place that could only hurt you further. It's important not to be vulnerable in unsafe places.

NO-WIN TRAP 3 AT WORK

You Have to Do Everything Yourself, and the Help You Do Get Is Never Enough

On the one hand, this issue appears rather simple. If you're the kind of person who always feels stuck doing everything yourself, stop. If it were that simple, however, obviously you would have done it already. So let's take a look at the conversations that may be taking place in your head that keep you from letting go and from feeling it's okay to get help:

"If anyone knows I need help, I'll lose my job."

"I'm tired of doing everything myself, but I'm the only one who does it right."

"I'm so busy doing everyone else's job, I never have time to do my own."

"By the time I train someone else to do it, I could have just done it myself."

"I really don't like this job, but I know they can't do without me."

"It's so hard to delegate work to anyone. I find it's just easier to do it myself."

"I don't need your input; I've got it figured out."

"Why is it that no matter how many times I ask you to do it a certain way, you act as if you never listen?"

"If people don't need me, what would I do with myself?"

"I just can't trust anyone else to do the job."

Breaking Free of No-Win Trap 3

Frankly, after reading the above lines, doing everything yourself actually can make a lot of sense. But unfortunately, over time, it can result in a lot of negative consequences:

- You feel exhausted.

- You feel resentful.

- You get no cooperation.

- Others call you a control freak.

- You work while you're sick.

- You never take a break.

- You feel guilty if you sit down.

- Others act abandoned if you take a day off.

- You're no fun to be around.

- You don't know if you can keep this up, but you can't stop either.

- You complain you have no one to lean on.

- You have no personal life.

- You're just too darn tired and you don't know how to change.

- You're afraid and you don't know how to make things different.

If any of these apply to you, it's totally understandable. Chances are, when you were a child, you had responsibilities that were beyond your years and were unable to trust and lean on those who should have been there. However, as time goes on, while you may look for those who can be there for you, the odds are you'll only attract those who want to lean on you, just as others have in the past. And so it is at work.

Consider the tips concerning jobs and interviewing at the end of this section and see if there are any you could try. Doing it all yourself is one of the most difficult habits to change, so we'll take it a little at a time. See if you can picture yourself saying or doing these things, just so you can take a first step. Before reading through them, recognize that there are people who successfully say and do these things and still manage to get the job done. The only difference between them and you is that they view the world as a place that really does have people there to help them. In fact, it even has *dependable* people who actually do come through very well.

Those with a sense of *basic trust and belief* that their needs will get met are more successful at delegating without constantly looking over their shoulder. These people know whom to ask, and recognize who will give them the results they want. They don't bother with those who say they'll come through but have proven they won't, over and over. They do not burden themselves with asking things of those who are not dependable. Successful delegators know whom to trust. They also trust their own ability to delegate.

Now consider the case of Marion, who discovers that she isn't all alone on the job and doesn't need to do it all herself.

Marion's Change of Heart—for the Better

Marion always wanted to head up a nonprofit agency. She'd worked at a number of them for years and finally got her wish. At the age of 47 she became director of an agency that had five divisions: adoption, domestic violence services, child-care-related services, job training, and meals on wheels. She had a manager underneath her for each one, an accountant, and a grant writer who specialized in the areas Marion had the most need for.

At first everything seemed to be going well. But as time went on, everyone noticed that whenever Marion delegated work to someone, before the day was through she'd be checking to see if they'd gotten it done or had at least gotten started. And if this wasn't annoying enough, she also never gave a realistic amount of time for the work, and would actually take the work back if she deemed it wasn't done quickly enough. If anyone had a good idea, either one-on-one or in a staff meeting, it would be shot down for some reason the boss always had in her back pocket. Most of the time, Marion would tell them they just couldn't understand because none of them could see the overall picture of the agency, and therefore their input wasn't helpful.

The five managers who worked for her became disgruntled, and because they had no success when they brought up their concerns to Marion directly, they began complaining among themselves. After a while the managers, and therefore their staffs, learned to just go through the motions and pretend they were working when they weren't. This actually seemed to satisfy Marion, as she then got to tell herself, and anyone who still cared to listen, that it all seemed to fall on her, and she was the only one who knew what she was doing. Then one day . . .

John, who had headed up accounting for years and was working late on a rare night for him, came into Marion's office, sat down across from her desk, and asked her how she was doing. Finding it impossible to hide her exhaustion—she was, as usual, working way past

8 p.m.—and admitting that she was coming down with the flu, Marion didn't have the energy to act as if she were on top of everything. Besides, being the only man who headed up a department, John didn't seem to be as threatening to her as the women.

Marion had grown up in a family of four girls, where her dad took potshots at everyone on a daily basis. It seemed that none of the girls could do anything right. The bottom line was that their dad was a raving alcoholic, and a lunatic at that. Everyone's job, including Mom's, was to make Dad appear like he was a great father and provider. In reality, he couldn't keep a job or maintain any structure as the head of the household. So, to keep him propped up, all four girls competed to see who could do everything best and who could stay out of the line of fire longest.

Being the eldest, and knowing that her mother was overwhelmed to the point of sleeping all the time, Marion took the brunt of her father's abuse, shielding everyone else while keeping it all together. No wonder she didn't trust anyone. She didn't have any reason or time to. She was too busy competing with her sisters, in the guise of protecting them, and trying to please a dad who couldn't be pleased. In truth, Marion did want to be helpful, and she did think it was her job to head up the family and protect her siblings.

Marion used to lie awake at night praying, and hoping that if she did everything "just right," Daddy would somehow become a "real man" and claim her as his favorite little girl. Mom would finally get out of bed, and her sisters would cheer her on.

Marion truly did the best she could as a young girl and did try to save their hopeless situation. She never realized, however, that in her efforts to help out, she was perceived by her sisters and her mom as wanting to take over. It felt to everyone but Marion that she was trying to outdo them and render them useless, just to get Dad to like her more. All that happened, of course, was that he expected more and more from her, and the rest of the family gave up trying to do anything but stay out of the way and avoid any contact with Marion.

She took her childhood story along with her to work. She couldn't relax at her agency job for five minutes. Always afraid "some woman" would take her place, she was afraid if she took a day off, she'd come back to an empty office. It had never occurred to Marion that perhaps the outer world might not be as harsh as life growing up in her family had been. She just assumed that because it was a dog-eat-dog world at home, it would be even worse in the business world.

She admitted to John that because she wanted her agency to work smoothly, she had to stay on top of everything all the time. She'd worked so hard to get to her position, she felt she would just die if she let everybody down. (What she didn't admit to John was her fear that she'd feel even worse if someone else took the agency over and did an even better job.)

John poured Marion a cup of coffee, poured one for himself, and then proceeded to do something Marion had never experienced before: he listened. He listened and she talked. She became vulnerable. Then John talked and Marion listened. Then they both sat still and said nothing for quite some time.

Marion had an epiphany then. She realized how much John was committed to the agency. As much as anyone, he'd helped build this entity and didn't want to see it go down the drain. Marion also finally understood that the five women managers were not out to get her. They just wanted to feel they were valuable as human beings and do their jobs.

She took an unusual leap of faith and asked John to help her run a staff meeting—where *he* actually conducted it and she got to sit back and listen. It frightened her to think she wouldn't have the reins of control, but she made the offer anyway. John happily agreed, and they both decided to have it the next week.

Marion lay in bed that night trying to decide which one of the managers would be most inclined to take potshots at her like her dad always had. But she was smart enough to realize that if she continued running the office her way, she would lose everything. So she finally fell asleep at about 4 a.m., thinking it was the best idea to simply have each manager bring notes and budgets to John to discuss what they needed to provide competent services. This would include what they needed from her in terms of support and delegation style. That was the scary part.

On the day of the meeting, Marion was nervous. She almost wore her most powerful-looking "day-in-court suit," but finally decided to wear something feminine and flowing, to suggest receptivity and a willingness to sit back. While this was all completely unnatural for her, she knew she'd have to change if everyone else was to respond well.

As the time for the morning meeting drew closer, Marion looked at herself in the mirror of her personal executive rest room and felt that somehow this time would be different. She trusted "the process" of letting others bring their best, and she knew that John already had a track record that proved he was there for the benefit of the agency. Perhaps, she thought, she was putting her trust in the right place this time.

Marion was moving in the right direction. She'd had an insight that she was not among vultures and pit vipers, and that everyone only wanted to do their job. In time she would develop the wisdom to know it was all just a matter of trust, observation, time, and a willingness to consider options and make changes when the signs come your way. Even if someone was out to give her a hard time, or to take something away from her, she still had options and could make changes.

Not everyone arrived at the meeting on time, and half of the managers left their notes back in their offices. When Marion began to show signs of frustration, John gave her a look that said, "It's all okay. We just have to put up with this behavior for now. The staff is trying to show you they're hurt and they don't trust bringing you their best work. They're afraid of getting shot down." Miraculously, without any words, Marion seemed to understand. She had a flashback about how she'd always stuck her neck out to try to answer Daddy's minefield questions when her sisters and her mom just sat back and watched her take the fall every time.

Inspired by compassion for her managers and staff, Marion began the meeting by thanking everyone for being there and for all their efforts on behalf of the agency. She then went on to acknowledge each person for what they were contributing. Ignoring the rolling eyes of disbelief and the glances back and forth across the room, she went on to say that at this particular meeting she would only listen, that John was going to conduct it, and each person would tell her what they found was going well in their department and what seemed to be giving them trouble—including her.

At first hardly anyone said much of anything. But as the meeting went on, and Marion demonstrated great maturity and an apparent ability to laugh at herself, most of the staff loosened up, and they ended the session with a discussion of how each department could better coordinate efforts and avoid duplicating services.

When the meeting was over, Marion was careful to set up a time to meet with each manager alone to go over what they needed, down to fine details. Marion closed the session by saying she was as surprised as everyone else that she could let go and even enjoy this sort of collaboration. And while it had been mentioned before, everyone was surprised that Marion had provided a wonderful lunch. As John had told her earlier, it would be the best spent money she ever authorized.

Everyone left in a much better mood, although there was certainly still some lingering doubt in the air. John told Marion that she'd done a great job, and she told him later that she finally understood that it was her responsibility to create an environment where her staff and managers could thrive. She realized that this would often mean supportively staying out of the way.

The last I heard, Marion had recently retired and left her agency very well funded and mostly in the hands of her same, high-functioning staff.

If feeling alone at work and letting go is what's most difficult for you, look around to see who can do what well. Acknowledge them for it, and then be willing to stand back and let them do it. Things might just get better. If they don't, you will have developed some valuable tools to use at your next job.

Five Tips for No-Win Trap 3

Stop Trying to Do It All Yourself at Work

1. *Ask about the help you'll have available to you on the job, right at the interview.* As much as you want the job, don't come on like

gangbusters promising to do the work of 20 people. It's low self-esteem to come across as if you can do it all single-handedly. In the long run you don't want a job where you have to be the Lone Ranger every day for the rest of your life. Once work expectations have been established, it's very hard to change them. Smart interviewees who tend to get the job and are respected in the long run will state right at the beginning what they can offer the company and what help they'll need to get the job done. If you don't ask for help then, you may never get it later on.

2. *Never give the job 150 percent at the start.* Leave yourself room to grow, and remember the saying, "The more you do that's not expected, the more they'll expect you to do."

3. *Do not confuse doing the job that's needed with feeling needed to do the job.* Be honest with yourself. Ask yourself if the work you're doing really needs to be done by *you* specifically, or if you're doing it to prove to yourself and others that you're really needed. There are people who feel they're not good enough unless they go overboard and do more than everybody else. Quite often those individuals are seen as nothing more than "control freaks." Do you work the way you do to get the job done, or do you do it to maintain your sense of control?

4. *Surround yourself with others who do exemplary work.* Rather than being afraid you'll lose your position if others are as competent as you are, free yourself up to do what you genuinely want, and you'll win yourself that promotion. Truly successful people can delegate well and surround themselves with competent people. If they can't, they're only seen as workhorses, deemed to always do the work for others and never receive the credit. You can't move upward and onward if you don't have others around who can take on that part of the job you either can't do or don't want to do.

5. *Take a fresh look at your job.* You're not in the same position you were as a child, overwhelmed with responsibilities. Make

a point of seeing your job as a new situation where the rules have actually changed. When you go to work tomorrow, look around you. Do you see the other employees there as children who don't get half as much work done as you do, or do you see them as colleagues or team players who are all in this together? Do you find yourself feeling you have to do it all? Is it possible you're still stuck in your old childhood thoughts and habits? If you are, that old line of thinking could be setting you up to continuously replay old patterns. If this is the case, when you go into work tomorrow, be someone who joins in with others rather than riding on top of them and taking over.

7

Decision Points

Wisdom is knowing which step to take next. Virtue is taking the next step.

David Starr Jordan

*I*nstead of always climbing out of one tough spot only to find yourself in another, picture living a life filled with "good feeling" choices. You *can* have such a life. In fact, I'll bet it's already starting. All you need is a little more help. This chapter is about making *choice* and *a genuine sense of overall well-being* your constant companions. It's also about how to stop feeling overwhelmed and defeated. Even more directly than before, you'll see that *how* and *when* you make your choices directly affects your overall well-being.

Clearly seeing the choices you have involves recognizing those places in your life where there is a sudden or gradual fork in the road. These "places" are key points that inevitably show up as you move closer and become more involved in a situation or a conversation, or when you step back to collect your thoughts and decide just how far you really want to go. These moments of decision demand that you either come forward with yourself or carefully back off.

The decision to lighten your load and generate more authentic well-being, or to add to the burdens and pressures on yourself, is one that is always yours to make. Remember, you are always accountable for who you are at any given time—even if it doesn't feel that way.

If you happen to be the parent of a teenager, it can be especially challenging to remember this. While teens are in the developmental stage of trying on identities and seeking out ways to exert what power they have, you may be grappling with who you really are and wondering if you ever had any real power anyway. This can be especially true if you're grappling with midlife issues yourself.

Holding your own with teens in your life, or with anyone for that matter, involves choosing whether or not to give them your fully authentic self at any given moment. You may feel, at this stage in your relationship, that the "real" you gets nowhere with them, or that you just don't feel safe revealing that part of yourself to them now. (It may be that they feel the same about you.) This could very well call for boundary setting and agreeing to be respectful of each other, even if there are issues each party disagrees about. It's important, at these times, to remain available and not insist that everything get settled immediately, all or nothing. There's no need to attempt to win with everybody all the time. In this instance, "winning" can mean that you and the "opposing party" are actually able to table particular issues for another round later, when a fresh approach and a different perspective is more possible, while agreeing to just get along for now.

You can decide if you want to exert more energy with someone and have a more honest conversation, or just sit back and let things blow over or cool down. Even though tension and pressure may be mounting inside, the choice is *still* up to you concerning which way to go. Often we succumb to these relentless pressures, believing we're actually making things better, or at least relieving some nagging sense of guilt.

However, the reality is, if you're making a comment or taking an action that is mainly motivated by pressure, you're not responding entirely out of "choice mode," where you have the clarity to sort through your options. Instead, you're reacting to lower the momentary tension, rather than effectively solving the dilemma that concerned you in the first place. This line of thinking may not be to your advantage, since what you say or do could in the long run become part of the problem.

To help you become more aware of opportunities for choice, this chapter has been divided into four sections based on the four stages, or four "decision points," of the basic no-win trap situation:

1. Recognizing when you're about to fall into a no-win trap

2. Recouping quickly after falling into a no-win trap

3. What to tell yourself if you're stuck in a no-win trap

4. Getting out of the no-win trap you're presently in

Let's turn now to the first major decision point. There's a good chance you're already becoming aware of the approach of a no-win trap. This section should help sharpen your awareness skills even further.

DECISION POINT I
Recognizing You're About to Fall into a No-Win Trap

We all have our Achilles' heal when it comes to no-win traps. Whether it's being taken for granted or taking others for granted, being easily hurt or being insensitive, being greedy or needy, going overboard or just plain being taken, all of us need to constantly remind ourselves of where our vulnerabilities lie.

Those who become "successful" learn how and when to make use of their energy, emotions, and capabilities. They also know how to develop, manage, and contain these capacities. Unfortunately, many of us never gain insight into those parts of us that are most dangerous and destructive, to ourselves and to others. These parts need constant supervision, or at least input from our objective inner observer, or from our friends, or even at times from psychotherapists. "Flaws," such as getting hurt too easily by a child's words or becoming angry if you aren't complimented enough, can seem harmless. But if too often you feel stung by these instances, and, in interpreting their meaning you begin to feel worthless about yourself, it can lead you to believe the world is a cruel and dangerous place, at least for you.

Below are listed 15 instances in which you might find yourself about to fall into a no-win trap. There are thousands of possibilities for this, but these 15 "entry points" should give you a good idea of what to be aware of. You might want to follow up with your own list of instances where you've fallen prey to a no-win trap in the past. You're bound to find yourself in similar places again, so you might as well make yourself aware of them now.

Three Tips on Avoiding No-Win Traps

Before we get started, here are three bonus tips that will help you fight off the seductive lure of no-win traps.

- *If in doubt, don't.* You have more power and choice in the matter *before* you put your all into something or start down a path in the wrong direction.

- *Beware of the first solution.* You know you're about to get yourself in a no-win trap when it occurs to you that your solution to the problem could actually add to it, or become another problem all by itself.

- *Know your weaknesses.* The more you are conscious and aware of your potential human sensitivities or challenges, and the sooner you step back and observe your situation, the less you'll be inclined to fall into a trap.

Fifteen Entry Points to a No-Win Trap

- You realize you're about to bite off more than you can chew.

- You start to promise something you don't want to promise.

- You realize you're starting to see someone more and more, when you know inside this is not the right person for you.

- You're trying too hard to make conversation with someone whom you'd rather just not be around.

- Once again you attempt to show love and care to your teenager by getting too obtrusively "into their space," when you realize that backing off and letting them know you're available would be better.

- You almost attempt for the hundredth time to get your mother-in-law to like you, even though you realize she'll *never* like anyone who had the audacity to try to take her son away.

- You start to fool yourself again by thinking that because you have credit left on your credit card, you actually have more money.

- You begin to refinance your house for the third time in three years because the rates are lower, then realize you'd also be giving your investment in equity away *again.*

- You start to mouth off at the one you love most because you're overloaded with frustration, then realize that this is the person you need to treat the best.

- You almost "party hardy" one more time, then realize you'll pay for it tomorrow.

- You start to beat yourself up for some mistake you made or for not being perfect, then wonder if you shouldn't give yourself some credit as well.

- Feeling angry and wanting to pick a fight, you consider calling the guy you've been seeing, even though you realize you're only feeling hurt because he hasn't called.

- You're upset about someone at work and about to gossip with your fellow employees to let them know what you *really* think about him.

- You want to tell off your ex because he or she is still such a jerk after all these years, even though their present behavior is why you left in the first place.

- You want to procrastinate one more day on an important project that's nearly due.

Hopefully, the clamp of the jaws in the no-win trap won't be biting you quite so frequently. For those times when you're slipping backward, and forgetting that you have choice in the matter, read on about Decision Point 2.

DECISION POINT 2

Recouping After Falling into a No-Win Trap

Although it's always wiser to avoid getting into a no-win trap in the first place, you have a second, very good window of opportunity to escape right after you've just fallen in.

Five Bonus Tips for a Quick Recovery

- *Avoid creating feelings of abandonment.* Fear of being abandoned is a primal human feeling that can lead a clingy person to ensnare you in a no-win trap. The longer you allow the person to grow dependent on you—for love, help, support, money, or whatever—the more difficult it will become to break off the relationship or alter it in some way that may not be amenable to them.

  Therefore, if you want the relationship to change or remain within certain limits—of time, duration, intimacy, dependency, etc.—you can avoid setting yourself up for a no-win trap by letting the other persons know as quickly as you can that you won't be able to be there for them. If you're honest up front, you'll save yourself, and them, much agony—and there's less of a chance that they'll take you for granted.

- *Don't put off the pain.* One of the least genuine reasons to keep someone hanging on to you when you don't want him or her in your life is because "you don't want to hurt them." There's a good chance they know how you really feel and they just haven't taken the initiative to talk about it, improve the situation, or break off the relationship themselves. But the longer you let a bad situation go on without addressing it, the more painful the hurt will be.

  If you're having a difficult time mustering up the courage to let someone or something go because you're afraid of the pain and hurt you might cause, it's entirely understandable.

But just remember: The pain you face today will be far less than what you'll face tomorrow.

- *Beware of guilt.* Guilt is another prison we hide in that keeps us from tending to our own needs and pulling out of a double bind. We should always try to be aware of the fact that where there's guilt, anger and resentment are sure to follow. And anger and resentment could lead you to do and say things that you'll *really* feel bad about down the line.

- *Be honest.* The key to stepping out of a no-win trap early on is honesty. That is, honesty first with yourself and then with others. Being honest from the beginning about what you can and can't do will generally keep you out of most no-win traps—a secret all too often learned only through experience.

- *Be conscious of your fear.* Fear may very well have been what snagged you. Perhaps it drove you to make a decision in haste, a decision that only added to your problems. The next time fear finds you, stop, sit, and wait. There's a good chance you'll get more information that way—without jeopardizing yourself further.

Now take a look at the following 15 suggestions for ways to help you quickly recoup when you've fallen into a no-win trap. If you have a difficult time using one or more of these suggestions, at least honestly converse with yourself regarding the reasons why. There's a good chance it has to do with one or more of the tips we just talked about above: You're willing to abandon your own needs to "save" someone from feeling abandoned; you don't want to hurt someone; you can't manage your guilt feelings; you're afraid; and/or you're having a difficult time being honest. Give yourself credit—this section is asking a great deal from you! It's where the rubber hits the road.

Often when I'm working with clients in this area, they tell me they find this very difficult. They say, "That's hard!" I agree. I often tell them, "We only do hard things in here." After a while, though, it gets easier, especially when you see the rewards for being more real, more who you truly are. Believe me. I'm doing hard things right now myself. It's worth it. *You're* worth it!

Fifteen Tips for Bouncing Back

- If you told someone you could do something that in truth you know is too much to take on, tell him or her that you just realized you have too much on your plate already, and so you'll have to pass at this time. Make it clear that you're informing them of this because you only just now realized that you couldn't do what they requested.

- When you feel you're on circuit overload, slow down rather than speed up, even though you're used to doing things the other way around.

- As for that budding relationship you've been erroneously cultivating? Try calling someone you trust, and role-play with them how to kindly bring the relationship to an end—before it gets any further along.

- When you notice yourself falling into old habits, or falling in with the "wrong people," go out of your way to find supportive people and positive activities that help to raise your sense of self-worth. If you notice you're in a no-win trap out of loneliness, acknowledge it. Then consider how much lonelier this situation will become down the road—especially when you feel trapped in it and it keeps you from being open to something more fulfilling. At least try to do other things besides seeing this person all the time. Try to wean yourself away through small steps.

- Do something you've always wanted to do, something that will generate feelings of generosity, appreciation, and fulfillment rather than resentment and anger. For example, you could consider volunteering at the nearby humane society or help give directions at a large medical complex. The crucial point here is to choose something that has meaning to you, that will engender a feeling of giving and receiving in a flowing combination.

- If you're trying to have a conversation with someone to patch things up, and you realize it's only going downhill, simply back away. Tell them you want to take a break or a time out, even if it's for a few minutes. Do not overly explain yourself, but apologize if it feels appropriate.

  Then, by all means, try not to get into any serious conversation with this person again, unless a major shift or opening for change seems to occur. They just can't do it, at least with you. Even if it appears that they can, the chances are high that they'll always come back to this same place with you. This individual may be more committed to making you wrong than to making the situation better.

  However, in the case of intimate relationships where your decision to make no more attempts to get closer could have grave consequences, the terms are different. Considering relationships with a spouse, where you can become stalemated and feel you can never win, another no-win situation of great magnitude could occur no matter what you do. If you're with someone you feel you can never get closer to, then you feel trapped if you stay. However, if you decide to leave, another trap occurs, causing divorce and havoc in its wake and possibly an inability to get through no-win traps with intimate relationships in the future. It's easy to believe the other person's inability to communicate is what's getting in your way. But if you have communication issues of your own that could be improved, it might well be that future relationships will come down to this again. Therefore, concerning no-win traps, it's always best to get new insights in your own communication concerning the relationship you're in right now. There is no time like the present to make changes.

For those of you who do not know which way to go at this time in your closest love relationship in your life, perhaps you could take a chance one more time, with a new angle and a willingness to listen, and try to make up rather than decide to leave.

- You've done it again—overused a credit card. This time, before it gets any worse, get help right away from a financial counselor or a bookkeeper. Find the help you need to develop good financial habits. Don't continue to try to manage money on your own when you know you need help.

- You tried too hard to please someone at work or in the family again, and in turn they treated you like a laughingstock and a fool. The next time you see them, be formal, cool, yet very civilized, and even kind if you can. At the same time, make the interaction as short as possible. Don't give them the opportunity to take you for a chump again.

- You've just upset the one you love the most because you're overwhelmed by work, children, money, and the world. This set him or her up to be cold to you and unavailable. Rather than waiting for it to blow over, apologize right away and let that person know you're making conscious efforts to maintain an air of respect and marriage etiquette. Then acknowledge them for all the wonderful things they've been doing and for how important they are to you. The second you take your loved ones for granted is the moment you begin to actively lose in your personal life, and other areas too.

- You actually partied again with old acquaintances you should have avoided like the plague. There is no intelligent advice to give you at this time, because when you're high, you aren't able to take good advice. However, in the aftermath, recognize this as a sign that you still haven't learned what you were meant to learn. Odds are, with each go-round the consequences will become more serious. It's amazing how far we're willing to go, and not use our own good judgment, out of the fear of making others feel rejected.

- You're mad at yourself for getting into a fight with your alcoholic husband again, a fight he then used to justify going out on another drinking binge. Rather than trying harder to keep the peace and please him, get yourself into Alanon and therapy, and recognize you have no power to change his drinking. Until you admit you're in a no-win trap, you have no chance of getting out of it. Pretending you have no responsibility for your own situation only keeps you stuck and blaming everyone.

- You called your boyfriend because you were upset that he didn't call you. Feeling put off, he said he just couldn't win with you. He went on to say that whatever he does, it's never enough. Rather than going on and on about how mad you are that he didn't call, honestly let him know that his calls are very important and reassuring to you. Tell him you need to hear from him once a day, at night, or once every other day, depending on what you need. Then say it's because you love to hear his voice. Ask him if it's all right with him if you call him if he doesn't call you.

  In today's "so connected world," the most consistently talked about issue is still telephone calls—who calls and who doesn't. Don't put yourself in a no-win trap if your guy doesn't always make that call. If having contact is what you need, call him. If he can't take that, let him go.

  P.S.: Only do this if you're in an established, mutually committed relationship. If you're still in the "getting to know you to see if I'm really interested" phase, wait it out or let go.

- You jumped in and got pushy about everything, to the point of putting the other party off again. Do your best to apologize, or just sit back and stop trying. Call someone you can talk to about this subject. Try to determine if this truly is a relationship where you may never have the opportunity for a satisfying conversation. If it is, back off.

If you can't effectively "keep your head out of the hornet's nest," it might be helpful to see a psychotherapist to talk things out, or even a psychiatrist to consider whether medication would help with impulse control and judgment issues. This is useful especially if you've had a pattern of jumping in too hard and being pushy with those who frustrate you.

- You've had it with your job, and you just called up an acquaintance from work to discuss how your boss may be feeling about you. This acquaintance may not have been the safest person to call, but you just had to talk to somebody! Go back into work tomorrow and smile. See how everything pans out. If the person you called tries to talk to you about it, thank them and then go about your business. Don't get into it further. They may be an "ally" today, but if you don't have that much history with them, and you're unsure about their coalitions in the office, they could end up being part of your problem. Wait it out. You can always look into what options you have for other jobs and start working on your résumé.

- You danced yourself into a corner and couldn't make a decision about which person to date, so now you're dating two different people. One is more trustworthy, and the other is more exciting. As much as you're enthralled with the exciting one, you have a feeling in your gut that you can't trust him. While you haven't formally committed to one or the other, you recognize that the more consistent one will most likely pull out if he discovers that you're seeing someone else.

At this point, sit back and see what happens. Perhaps you can just slow down the train a bit and be less available for a while. Give yourself time to see how everything unfolds. Don't feel you have to make any hasty decisions. If you feel you have to rush, take that as a sign that something isn't quite right.

Now the plot thickens. Time passes, you let down your guard, forgot about the previous advice, and suddenly find yourself hurtling down the double-bind highway to nowhere. Before you get lost any further, it's time to slow down, take a look around, and find yourself the right off-ramp.

DECISION POINT 3
What to Tell Yourself If You're Stuck in a No-Win Trap

At this point you have yet another chance to escape. You can decide if it's your fate in life to stay stuck on the endless road you're on, or you can start looking for an exit sign. Believe it or not, the choice is still up to you.

Changing roles can be much more difficult than changing lanes on a freeway, but it can be done if you're determined enough. The theory is basically the same. When you change lanes, you turn on your signal and aim in the direction you intend to go. Sometimes the traffic is so thick you have to wait a while, but you stick to it. When you change *roles*, you have to first picture yourself in the other role—imagining, for instance, that you're someone who can make a decision without being afraid of how others will respond.

You must be willing to hold fast to this picture of yourself, even if no one else gets it. With changing roles, just like when you're driving down the highway and other cars don't seem to want to let you in, you have to stick to your intent. Keep in mind your determination, your commitment to the change, and the timing. It's truly up to you.

There are people who would never think of driving anywhere but in the slow lane. There are those who have convinced themselves they will only drive on surface roads. We have an amazing way of doling out our limits as if someone else gave them to us.

If you've been a "fix-it" person, and your only concept of an identity or purpose in life is to be seen as that, you may decide to continue to stay where you are—and probably also continue to steadily sink deeper. If you're a "scapegoat," you could continue to stick your neck out and be the one to always take the blame. You might even tell yourself you like the role. If you've been a "martyr," and being the sole sacrifice for the family is how you get recognition, you may have to learn to go without recognition while you tend to your own needs for a change.

Being happy with yourself—independent of the approval of others—is the foundation for choice and freedom in your life. When you wake up with a more peaceful heart, more peace will eventually come from others. Some of them will give it, some of them won't. You have to be willing to let go of those who don't. *Sometimes you have to lose others in order to gain yourself.*

It's only when you recognize your own worthiness that you can begin to climb out of a no-win trap. Once you've determined that you truly do deserve better, it's helpful to remind yourself with clear statements about who you are and what you want from life.

Here are 10 self-statements to help steer you away from the habitual actions that keep you stuck, and to help carry you forward in a new direction. Read them over carefully and determine which ones are the most useful to you. Commit to saying them over and over to yourself for at least a week. Believe what you say and say what you mean.

Ten Positive Self-Statements

- The "right way" in this situation is for me to recognize the importance of my own needs and well-being. I am committed to making sure my needs get met. I will do my part, I will not "drain" others, and I will ask for help from those who are willing and able to give it.

- Nothing good can come from this much suffering. For my own mental health and for my survival, I will cut my losses and stop supporting this impossible situation. Accepting the loss is far better than endlessly bearing the pain.

- It's better to wait for what I really want than to settle for something I don't. I will end this relationship once and for all; it's dragged on far too long.

- People will say what they may, but I refuse to take the blame for this situation any longer. I know what really happened here, and I recognize the part I played. I'll spend no more energy trying to explain.

- Starting right now, I will no longer pretend that this unworkable situation can be resolved. It's better to step out and start over than to keep on nagging and demanding change. The only changes I can make are changes in myself.

- Just because this feels familiar doesn't mean it's good or safe for me. I'm ready to start in a new direction, moving slowly forward. I'll check in with myself along the way to see what feels right and what feels wrong. I am not looking for "better" than what I had—I'm looking for what's "good" for me.

- This dilemma is not my responsibility and it never really was. It's not up to me to fix everyone's problems just because they assume I will. It's my job to take care of myself.

- I'll spend no more energy feeling devastated and disappointed that those I counted on have turned on me. I'll pick myself up and keep going. I will learn everything I need to learn so as not to be vulnerable in unsafe places again. I will not be bitter. Instead, I'll use the good judgment and self-honesty I hadn't been using in the past.

- I will no longer let others mistreat me as a way to make up for my past mistakes. I will be treated with respect and with appropriate boundaries, and refuse to engage if those boundaries are broken.

- I will love myself the way I want others to love me. I can't expect anyone else to treat me any better than I treat myself. I'll be responsible and respectful toward myself. I will not indulge myself to try to make up for the past.

After reviewing the above statements and choosing those that best apply to you, read on to Decision Point 4. It will help you find your footing in a life that's far more fitting.

DECISION POINT 4
Getting Out of No-Win Traps You're In Now

If the trap you're in now is a substantial one, finding a way out can be daunting. This may be at least part of the reason you've stayed in your particular dilemma as long as you have. Your situation could be complicated with logistical, financial, health, emotional, or any number of other problems. It's generally best, therefore, to detach from the situation one step at a time, so you don't feel further overwhelmed or traumatized in the process of trying to extract yourself.

Your first step should be to list all the issues and problems you're dealing with, so you can begin to distinguish and disentangle each component part of the trap in order to better see what's actually taking place. Try to work with one part at a time if possible.

If you have both emotional and physical changes to make, such as moving and leaving those you're attached to, begin detaching yourself emotionally first. If your circumstance is mainly emotional and your stomach is all in knots, make it a priority to deal with those issues most directly connected with this emotional state. It's easy to let yourself get muddled into a frenzy when you discover you're in an emotionally laden no-win trap; you can forget to take care of your most basic needs, which is probably what landed you in the no-win trap in the first place. Allowing you to get even more run-down will only make the trap that much harder to escape.

Getting help from friends, and seeing an M.D., chiropractor, nutritionist, psychotherapist, and/or a personal trainer can help you be in the best shape to face what you have to do. It also gives you support so that you're not facing it *alone*. There are many avenues for help and insights today, and you can tailor your list of potential resources to fit your own particular needs. You can choose from various types of psychotherapy, massage or meditation programs, spiritual centers and churches, neurolinguistic programming, medical intuitives, weekend workshops, personal coaches, support groups, adult education classes, prayer groups, retreats, or even just getting away to a beautiful place in nature. The trick is to open yourself up to new experiences while staying in tune with what feels right to you. The more you're willing to find out what's available and let others know you need help, the less time you'll spend in a no-win experience.

People in perpetual no-win traps tend to isolate themselves from others and attempt to carry their burden all on their own. While they say they don't want to be a burden to others, what they're really doing is not letting others in. It's one thing to gripe to the world about your dilemma; it's another thing entirely to try to get some help for it.

If you're convinced your situation cannot be rectified in any way, recognize that it's only a feeling you have, a perfectly understandable feeling. But just because you don't have an answer for your dilemma doesn't mean there isn't one available to you. Looking back, I'm amazed at the dilemmas I've somehow gotten through that at the time I was sure even Houdini couldn't escape.

I sometimes picture a helicopter flying overhead (which is not too hard to picture these days), and know it can see more of what's down the road than I can at that moment. I know that if I'm just willing to keep my chin up and look skyward, an answer of some sort will eventually come to me. It will come, that is, when I'm ready to receive it, when I'm willing to believe it's there.

When you feel yourself caught in a no-win trap, beware that any new or additional request made of you could make things even worse. Recognize that you do have choice in the matter. Everyone needs to draw his or her own line in the sand. Otherwise, there's no telling how bad things can get.

REVIEW YOUR NO-WIN TRAP COMPONENTS

Here are the basic components of a no-win trap as we laid them out in Chapter 1. Consider how they relate to your current dilemma.

1. You feel trapped by a conflict or problem. You're convinced you can neither escape nor win the battle.

2. Despite this, you feel compelled or have a strong sense of responsibility to do something to solve the problem.

3. You believe you can't have a successful conversation with the person you need to talk to the most. That person is convinced the problem lies entirely with you, and approaching them only seems to make matters worse.

Before we go further, compare these components with the list of issues that make up your own no-win trap, and pick out those problems you most want to focus on for the rest of this chapter. Or, if you prefer, just read on and see what comes up for you. You may find yourself altering your stance on some issues, while other concerns may come to the forefront.

FIRST STEPS

When you're trapped in the jaws of a no-win trap, it's important not to make any changes until you fully recognize that the way you've been operating must come to a stop. That realization will propel you to take the necessary steps to move forward toward freedom of choice and a healthier lifestyle for you and those you love.

In the case below, you'll see the steps one woman took to calm the "chattering monkeys" in her head and extract herself from a no-win trap that might easily have swallowed up her and her family. She'd been dealing with the situation for a long time but was determined to keep it from getting any worse. Even though she initially felt her situation was hopeless, by doing things differently than she'd done before, she ultimately found a way to win. Thanks to her determination, and her willingness to get help and to follow her vision step by step, she was able to finally get her needs met—along with everyone else's needs.

Diane Finally Gets Her Man and Kevin Finally Holds His Own

Diane was truly in a dilemma. From her point of view, her husband had always seemed too close to his mother. It was bad enough when Kevin insisted on bringing her along on their family vacations, but now his mother was threatening to actually move into their house.

Kevin explained that his mom, Patti, could take care of the kids, allowing the two of them to go out at night, as an adult couple, alone. But Diane knew that his mother would make sure that never happened; that she would end up escorting Kevin, her, and the kids wherever they went.

She and Kevin had married in their early forties, and Kevin had still been living with his mother. Diane's friends had repeatedly warned her, but she was so delighted with the way Kevin financially and emotionally cared for her children, Dawn and Carmen, from her previous marriage, that it never occurred to her that he wouldn't be willing to part with his mother.

A year had passed since Kevin had moved Diane and her two daughters into a condominium complex he'd had built and owned. It was four blocks from the house where his mother still lived. The only thing that kept Diane from feeling that Patti wasn't living right on top of them was the fact that this was San Francisco, and those four blocks were extremely steep. Patti no longer felt up to driving in the city, and the high-grade hill kept her from walking over.

Somehow, Diane and Kevin managed to grow closer even though Kevin continued to cater to his mother's neediness. When his mom's health took a turn for the worse, the juggling he went through became even more of a strain. Patti refused to consider outside help, and when Diane suggested to her mother-in-law that sometimes she would come to her house to help instead of Kevin, so he could take a break, Patti said she only wanted her there if she brought the kids.

There was no way around it for Kevin. He felt stuck, and so did Diane. Kevin's father, George, had died when Kevin was very young. Being an only child, and an overly responsible one at that, Kevin had taken it upon himself to care for his mother. It never occurred to him that his mother was running his life until Diane pointed it out and began reminding him of the fact on a daily basis.

Kevin became locked in a troubling no-win trap. If he tended to his mom, Diane felt slighted; if he tended to Diane, his mom began to whine.

Kevin and Diane came close to losing each other after their second year together. After much coaxing from Diane, who promised not to nag if he'd join her in marriage counseling, they began attending sessions together. It seemed to help.

Things soon took a turn for the worse, however. Kevin's mother could no longer live by herself, and one day she called, crying, to beg Kevin to let her move in. It was Diane who answered the phone, however, and all she could say after listening was, "He'll have to call you back."

She stood in the kitchen ready to scream. She'd put up with so much already—from Patti's meddling over what color to paint the house, to what to do on the kids' birthdays. Kevin had promised that his mother would never move in with them, but when push came to shove, she knew he'd cave in. Diane felt trapped in a no-win situation, convinced she could neither escape nor win.

Now, caught in this seemingly intractable double bind, she felt helpless and unable to do anything about the situation. She knew that when she told Kevin about Patti's request, it would be impossible to have a successful conversation with him. His heartstrings and apron strings would be so tied together that her own needs would never be heard. Yet she still felt that to keep her family life together, and to retain her own peace of mind, she had to do *something*, and her timing had to be just right.

Step One.   She decided to list the various issues involved, and to decide which one she was most committed to doing something about. She listed her issues this way:

1. It was clear that her mother-in-law could no longer take care of herself.

2. Kevin would feel responsible.

3. His mother would do just about anything to move into the same condominium the family lived in.

4. There was barely enough room for everyone as it was.

5. Just the thought of living with her mother-in-law made Diane fly into a rage.

6. Diane believed that her relationship with Kevin would be over if his mother moved in. She also realized how much she loved Kevin and didn't want to lose him.

Diane became committed to doing whatever it took to make sure Patti would not move into the household with them. While she told herself she was willing to lose Kevin over this, she believed that if she thought things out, she could keep her mother-in-law from moving in and somehow keep her husband too.

Step Two. Before calling Kevin, Diane thought about what options were available to her. She came up with the following three:

1. She could call Kevin and let him have it! She'd let the chips fall where they would, and she'd check herself into a weeklong retreat for women, held just outside of San Francisco.

2. She could research assisted-living places in San Francisco that might offer a variety of services for Patti, including ongoing care and access to the companionship of neighbors she would sorely miss if she left them behind completely.

3. Kevin could house his mom in the condominium that was for sale two doors down, and hire someone for assisted living whether Patti liked it or not.

After coming up with these possibilities, Diane knew she'd better calm down first, so she could pick out the best one. She was wise enough to know that Kevin was always easier to deal with when he didn't feel stuck between her and Patti. Diane fixed herself a cup of coffee and considered the situation.

Step Three. What was the best thing that could happen here?

It occurred to her that this dilemma actually had some possibilities that could work in her favor. Her children liked seeing Patti. Dawn was now 8, and though she would never practice piano for Diane, she did like to play for Patti. Besides, Patti enjoyed having Dawn over to her house.

Diane envisioned Dawn practicing piano at Patti's house a few doors up (if she stayed in a condo), or visiting Grandma in an assisted-living facility.

Step Four.   Diane considered the worst that could happen, and pictured her mother-in-law moving into her and Kevin's very own bedroom. She was tired of hearing Patti say, "Oh, every time I look in Kevin's eyes, he reminds me how much I miss my late husband, George." Diane decided it was not a good idea to think too hard about the worst thing, but decided she would stand firmly by her "line in the sand." If push came to shove, she was prepared to tell Kevin that she'd move out if Patti moved in. But not before she did her best to convince him that Patti living with them would be the worst of several far superior options.

Step Five.   Diane decided she needed to know the details on the options she would present to Kevin before she got on the phone with him. She took out the phone book and began making calls. She found out the prices, insurance requirements, and activities at 10 different assisted-living retirement homes in the area. By noon she narrowed it down to the best possible choice, as she landed on one that had competitive bridge tournaments, bringing retired people in from all over the area. Patti might not be able to walk well, but she could still play a mean game of bridge.

Step Six.   Diane moved to the next step in her plan—to resolve the situation by making allowances for contingencies and receiving feedback from others. She was determined to show Kevin there were reasonable and actually better alternatives to having his mother move in.

Putting her own hurt feelings aside, Diane promised herself she would try to remain objective and keep the emotional jockeying out of the equation. Deep down she knew Kevin loved her every bit as much as his mother, and even more. She was determined to present solutions to Kevin without denigrating his mother, and to point out how he could benefit, as well.

Step Seven.   Diane acknowledged to herself that so far she was handling the situation coolly and calmly. Had this been a year ago, she knew she would have hung up on Patti and angrily called Kevin, telling him, "It's between me or your mother! You'd better get it right this time!" She was proud of her evolving communication skills.

She contemplated, then, how she would broach the subject with Kevin. She decided to cook him his favorite meal, remind him of how proud she was that his growing number of building projects were going so well, and tell him that she didn't even mind that he was working longer days. (She figured a few brownie points couldn't hurt. Besides, the more Kevin was reminded of how much he already had on his plate, the better the chances that he might not want to take on one more problem.)

Diane decided she would tell him after dinner, when the kids were occupied. She planned to begin by saying, "Mom called and realized she can't live alone anymore. I told her you'd call her this evening. But before you do, I want to let you know that I've done a little research. I found 10 wonderful assisted-living retirement complexes, and some of them have bridge tournaments."

She planned to let it go from there and see what emotional attachment or detachment would come from Kevin. Diane thought she would add that she knew how wonderful Kevin was and that he would certainly do the right thing. Only if necessary would she tell him how important it was to her that Patti shouldn't live with them. As soft as men can be sometimes with their own mothers, she was sure Kevin knew how strongly she felt about that.

Step Eight.   Diane proceeded to calm her mind with positive self-statements such as: "I know I will get my needs met in this world, and no matter how anyone else acts, I will stay calm. That way, I'll be more conscious about the next step I need to take."

The rest of the afternoon, she made dinner and set the table, with more thought about every detail than she ever had before. It would be a sure sign for Kevin that something was up, but he always fell for her BBQ spareribs and homemade spice cake. After all, she used his mother's recipes.

Step Nine.   While setting the stage and preparing dinner, Diane talked on the phone with supportive friends to give her a better sense of herself and of her roles in life.

That evening, Kevin got home early. He walked in and immediately said, "Gee, it smells great. What's going on in here?" Diane gave him a warm hug, and Kevin knew he was heading for trouble. But he didn't mind too much. He realized how much he loved his wife, and that he wanted to put her first.

"I need your help," Diane began. She told him about the phone call from his mother and the fact that Patti could no longer live on her own.

Kevin said, "I knew this would come up soon. I remember telling Mom soon after Dad died that she would never have to worry, and I would always take care of her. I promised her early on she would never have to live in an old folks home and die by herself."

Diane felt herself growing woozy. The only thing that kept her from falling off her chair was that she'd promised herself she would remain calm. She silently said within, "Be quiet. You haven't heard everything he has to say."

Kevin went on. "So I've been thinking. One of the condos is up for sale. It actually is set up so two people could live there. I could put an ad up to see if another elderly person would like to move in along with my mother, and we could see what benefits she has that allow for assisted living. It's a good thing, Diane, that you made me sign my mother up for long-term nursing care insurance. That gives us options, and I won't have to let her down. I'll call her after dinner, and when she starts crying about wanting to live with us, under the same roof, keep cheering me on so I don't back down."

Diane sat there in amazement. Not only was she happy she heard the very words she'd wanted to hear from Kevin, but she was also impressed with herself for keeping her mouth shut and giving Kevin a chance to talk.

After dinner, Kevin called his mother and laid it all out for her: to choose between moving into one of his condos, hopefully with another person, or moving to a place set up for assisted living. He didn't even give her a chance to speak. She told him she'd prefer the condo. Kevin told her he loved her and would get working on it right away.

That night, Kevin and Diane went to bed especially early. For the first time in weeks, they made passionate love. Diane felt so happy that she'd finally gotten her man. And Kevin felt as if he'd just become one.

You might think this no-win trap has an unusually positive ending. While it does, more and more people are catching on to how to do it. They are realizing that you can't very well get out of a corner if you're constantly putting someone else in one. The more you invite others to see how they'll benefit in a situation, and the more you follow the nine steps above, the more you'll be able to finally beat your no-win trap.

Consider some of the positive things Diane did to help her situation along. It's actually a good idea to follow them in all your interactions, and to develop preparations to deal with coming traps. When you do reach a point of no return, and you need to make some major changes or head off a growing problem, you'll have stored up emotional as well as financial resources that will allow you to do what needs to be done. For example:

- Because she knew she was in a no-win trap, Diane had stopped nagging about the situation a while back, realizing she'd never win that way.

- Making sure Kevin's mother had nursing home insurance helped give the family options, and cut off several inroads for Patti's manipulation. Diane helped Kevin see how he was protecting everyone by doing this.

- Diane considered timing; she didn't act on impulse or anger.

- Diane listened to Kevin after presenting her thoughts. Although she was willing to play her final card (moving out herself), she waited to hear everything from the other side first. She knew what she was committed to, and conveyed that more by her actions than her words. She also conveyed her commitment to her husband and her family, and worked to make it so her husband would be willing to listen.

Your own happy endings may take longer than Diane's. Some of them could even involve walking away and starting over. The most important aspect to keep in mind is that, whatever happens, you'll be moving closer to being true to yourself, and to everyone involved, for that matter. Believe it or not, it's possible for all of us to live a life of genuine choices, without constant feelings of doom. The next chapter is dedicated to your staying out of no-win traps and becoming more your own true self.

QUICK-CHECK CHATTERING MONKEYS EXERCISE
For Getting Out or Staying Out of No-Win Traps

Consider the following points as you contemplate what to do in a no-win trap dilemma, or a situation that could easily develop into one:

1. Consider your issues. Pick the one you're most committed to following through on all the way at this time.

2. What ways can you deal with it? Think of at least three. That will help you see you have options.

3. What is the best that could happen? Play your thoughts all the way out in your mind.

4. What is the worst that could happen? The worst almost never happens, but it helps you to consider contingencies. Concerning present or future "worst case scenarios," the key point is to remain open to help and input, especially in those moments when you're sure nothing will work.

5. Is there some person or service you can consult? Make good use of outside input. Remember that the final decision is up to you.

6. Consider your overall plan to resolve the situation, while making allowance for contingencies and feedback from others. Remember, what you ultimately think is what counts.

7. Decide if you'll act now, later, or do nothing. Sometimes just standing back for a while is the best thing.

8. Calm your mind with positive self-statements such as, "I can deal calmly and effectively with the consequences of this decision."

9. Surround yourself with supportive people and organizations that can help provide structure while you make changes and move on to new things in life. Create a list of names and phone numbers of people you can call upon.

Once you've gone through all of the above nine steps, decide what you'll focus on next, beyond your no-win trap dilemma, and keep that focus as much as possible. Dwelling on your problems all the time can often do more harm than good. Do all that you can do, then let some help and answers come to you. In the long run, what really counts is the inner belief that you'll find an effective and positive way to get through and out of your situation.

8
Living a Trap-Free Life

The duty to be alive is the same as the duty to become oneself, to develop into the individual one potentially is.

Erich Fromm

Living the "good life," free from being constantly stuck in a jam or pulling yourself out of no-win situations, is not about "having it all" or "just being lucky." It's about making good choices and realistic decisions at the time they need to be made. Living a trap-free life requires you to recognize that change is ongoing and inevitable. It's about knowing you deserve good things, and recognizing that there's a way for you to have a satisfying existence that doesn't depend on the approval of others.

You can either guide your "inner raft" with a well-centered rudder or wait for the tide to take you where it will. Even when it's not apparent, the choice is always yours. Either you'll proactively alter your course when the need presents itself, or some crisis will eventually alter it for you.

Most of us don't like change and conflict. We try to live somewhere between being proactive and being overwhelmed. But change is inevitable, and at some point down the road we'll inevitably come face-to-face with our base conflicts. The more we have our "ear to the ground" and "our eyes to the horizon," listening and watching for the hidden clues in ourselves and in others, and the subtle changes required to steer a proper course, the less chance we'll have of a head-on collision. We will simply come to see that altering our course is a natural part of existence, rather than an insult to our rutted way of thinking.

You can't sit there and say nothing because you don't want to rock the boat, and then expect others to know what you're thinking. You also can't blow up and then expect others to respect or even listen to you later on. By the same token, you can't expect to repeatedly tell someone the same thing over and over and expect that they'll eventually do what you say because they said they would, just to shut you up.

If you don't like the response you're getting, say or do something else. If others won't change, you'll have to. Quite often we find ourselves nagging others to alter their behaviors because we don't want to bother altering our own. Even if we're "right," change won't come about from others if they personally see no reason to change. Make sure you aren't part of the problem in the mix of your own double bind.

If "doing nothing" is a major change for you, it could be the way for you to go right now. On the other hand, if you never step up to the plate, perhaps now is the time to do so.

Life has a way of showing us what works and what doesn't. Make sure you're someone who is genuinely committed to getting what you really want and need. It is so subtle, seductive, and easy to fall into the trap of proving life will never work out for you. Feeling sorry for yourself is very catchy, especially if it gets you some form of attention from those who generally look the other way.

Make sure you're not your own worst no-win trap. Look within to see if you could possibly be double-binding yourself or those around you. You know you're doing it when you put yourself in a situation where you just can't win, and you insist on staying there. For example, there's nothing sadder and more pathetic than trying to get the love and acceptance of someone who just isn't interested in loving you back, at least not the way you want them to. If that has been you, you still have time to change.

Either find a way to receive the love they do have to give you, or let them go altogether. The only thing you have to give up is the way you've been approaching your situation. It's not even like anything is "wrong;" it's just that if you haven't been experiencing life the way you want to, you need to alter your approach or be stuck in the no-win trap you've created. There's plenty of love and opportunity available to you in this world. Spend more time focusing on what there is for you, rather than on what there isn't. Sometimes there's no greater joy than finally cutting your losses and discovering who you are. Life's too short to live in agony.

Being mad at someone because they aren't the same as when you met them 20 years ago is as ludicrous as insisting an oak tree not grow out of its original pot of soil. Change is a given factor in the natural course of life. It's not a personal affront to you.

For those of us who don't like conflict or confrontation, we'll need to be ready to change early on, and be comfortable with giving ourselves input and taking feedback from others. If you're together in the same household with a person who never rewraps the bread when they make themselves a sandwich, lovingly let them know they need to change the habit. Don't wait to tell them about it as you're throwing them out of the house for being a slob. Telling people how you feel about a situation when it immediately occurs will save you many no-win traps in your life. Leaving situations "to the benefit of the doubt" is the surest route to anger and miscommunication.

At the same time, if the new love of your life reminds you to put the bread back in the fridge well-wrapped, see that as their way of investing in you and letting you know what they need from you so you can happily coexist for a long time to come. Refrain from asking them to tell you everything they don't like about you and how you're just never good enough. Just hug them and say, "Thanks for telling me."

Give and receive. It's that simple. That's all successful living requires. Just as you can't inhale without exhaling, you have to give from your genuine self if you want to get anything genuine back. On the one hand, if you only give out energy and orders, you can't expect others to just take it from you graciously and not become resentful. On the other hand, you can't just sit there and expect others to do all the work. It's a two-way street.

If you've been inclined to live your life like a donkey waiting around for the carrot, justifying that your discomforts are worth the few rewards available to you, it's time to recognize that a feast is waiting for you somewhere in the world. You no longer have to dine on crumbs. There may well be a way to have more effective give and take in the situation you're in, but if you've tried every angle and run out of ideas, you may do well to begin looking elsewhere.

For those who've been the consummate "fix-it person," going along at your usual frenetic pace trying to patch everything up and force it into a tidy bundle, it's time to stop and, with more ease and authenticity, enjoy everything that has always been waiting for you. You can't have force and authenticity taking place at the same time.

This may require you to simply "let go," allowing the chips to fall where they may. In the long run, it can be much better than pushing things to the breaking point.

And then there's our scapegoat, our would-be hero, always hoping that the light at the end of the tunnel is the answer that will save us all, and not just an oncoming train. If you find that this is you, it's time to put down your burden and simply save yourself. You're wonderful just the way you are, and there's nothing you need to prove to others. You will not help your situation by thinking you need to be someone "more" or "less" than you are.

For those of you who are bravely altering your martyrlike behavior and beginning to take better care of yourself, try to remember on a daily basis how important it is for everyone involved that you meet your own needs first. Just as they tell you on an airplane, in the event of an emergency, first put the oxygen mask on yourself before helping those next to you. This is true even if those next to you are your own children. If you want to be available to others, you must first take care of yourself. Then you can give "of yourself" to others, rather than "give up" yourself for others. That's the difference between freedom and a no-win trap.

THE SECRET OF FREEDOM

Every time you find yourself in a no-win trap, be aware that you've given up a piece of the real you in some way, at least momentarily. On the other hand, whenever you feel you are "just being yourself," and you're filled with a sense of well-being, *no matter what's going on,* you know the real you is expressing itself, with no need for explanation.

You know it when you feel it, and you feel it in your heart. It's the sensation of putting out energy that doesn't feel squashed or taken away. You feel a sense of satisfaction coming back to you. The feeling is one of *trust*. Yes, trust.

Trust is the secret ingredient of freedom. The more you trust that you have a right to have your needs met and that you ultimately will have them met, the less you'll find yourself in no-win traps.

It doesn't even have to be about a major event. "Trust" is in part the experience that you have when looking at a beautiful sunset, or even some more ordinary sight, and you suddenly stop and feel in your bones that you yourself are an inherent part of the living cosmos. *You belong.* You are not hovering around the edges, convinced you'll never fit in. You're part of the flow. You count, and not necessarily because you're even doing anything, but simply because you're being who you are.

You count because you exist. You can "trust" that you are an integral part of some larger process that has been created in part by you; and you are "on your way"—not that you're even "going anywhere," but that you're *a part* and not *apart*.

You're not on the outside looking in. You have the freedom to choose, to commit, and to stay in something that's very important to you. You finally have the feeling inside that you no longer need to run or leave if "only you had the chance." You don't need to escape some trap. You are home. You are safe.

In contrast, when you're giving up who you are, your energy and efforts feel blocked. Listen to your inner conversation—that's the one that counts. As you get closer and closer to listening to who you really are from within, you'll no longer be "stuck" in someone else's idea of how things should be, while you dream and want and crave. You'll no longer be held hostage, holding everything up for a need or dilemma that you never truly wanted in the first place. You'll belong. You'll belong in a way so you can also belong to and with others, as you choose, because you'll feel seen, heard, witnessed, understood, accepted, loved, acknowledged, and satisfied. You will get your needs met, and you'll finally be yourself.

And who exactly are you?

One way to think about it is to look ahead to the end of your life and imagine yourself looking back. The following "newspaper article" exercise will help you see who you are and where you'd like your life to go from here.

WHO DO YOU WANT TO BE FOR THE REST OF YOUR LIFE?

Although it's been said, "Life is what happens to you when you're making other plans," you're less inclined to be thrown off course by a no-win trap if you have a picture of how you'd like your life to go. The more solid your vision, the less likely you'll get thrown off track. You're sure to take some unexpected journeys, but in the long run there's a path we all follow that is inherently our own.

Imagine you're 95 years old, looking back at your life. A major newspaper is featuring an article about you. What would you like to have written about you? What could you say about any forks in the road? Consider the following questions and add anything else you'd like. The closer you stay to the story you believe is the real you, the smoother sailing you'll have ahead.

- What would you say has been your greatest accomplishment?

- Did you follow your dreams?

- What challenges have you overcome?

- What ideas, things, people, and places have you cherished?

- What situations did you learn to stay away from?

- What regrets have you worked through?

- What compromises have you made?

- What people have you forgiven?

- What possible changes were you hoping to make?

- Did you make the changes you hoped to?

- What is the legacy you've left?

- What was your favorite part of your life?

- What could you say you're doing right now, if anything, to help make this present part of your life one of the best parts?

- Whose lives did you make easier?

- Who did you let into your life to make things easier for you?

- What gifts did you receive from others?

- What gifts did you give to others?

And most of all:

- What no-win traps did you leave behind?

- What no-win traps did you avoid altogether?

- What did you learn from the no-win traps that still tugged at you and at times even won?

When you're done answering these questions, take a look at the following points designed to help you live your life as authentically as you can, while avoiding as many no-win traps as possible.

28 STEPS TOWARD A NO-WIN-TRAP-FREE LIFE

1. Know your true self.

2. Commit to being true to your self.

3. Live in such a way that you can sleep easy at night, without letting "feeling guilty" rule your decisions.

4. Reckon with guilt feelings. If you truly are "guilty" about something and you can do something about it, then take honest steps to rectify what you've done. If you can't honestly do anything about it, hold your head up, keep going, and do not ruin the rest of your life.

5. Be able to feel good about the choices you make, even if others are not.

6. Know where you stand on the scale of 1 to 10 every day, so you know when you can take on more and when you can't (see Chapter 4).

7. When you see a potential trap on its way, you don't always need an immediate answer. Give yourself time to step back and decide how to deal with the situation. If you're not sure which way to go, jump down to tip number 12 and go from there.

8. Know when to say yes and when to say no.

9. Let people know right away when you've bit off more than you can chew and you can't be there for them.

10. Think ahead so you have options you like, rather than being stuck and upset no matter what you do.

11. Nip your potential problems in the bud, even before they are problems. At least nip your problems before they nip you.

12. Do the Chattering Monkeys exercise from Chapter 7 whenever your thoughts get confusing or just too much to handle.

13. If you have a persistent dilemma, get help.

14. If you have a dilemma, deal with issues as a situational no-win trap and take everything step by step as much as possible. Learn not to let your emotions overwhelm you when there's nothing you can do about the situation. Know whom to talk to for support and to just feel heard, and whom to talk to for solid solutions.

15. If in doubt, shrink a molehill down to nothing, rather than making it into a mountain.

16. If you're bored, do something fun and creative, rather than nit-picking and griping.

17. If a problem occurs, think positively that your needs will get met, rather than believing you'll be doomed.

18. Do not confuse "familiar" with "good." If you need to go outside the realm of what you know to improve your situation, get help from those who have been there and blaze a new trail for yourself.

19. Make no attempt to change the opinions of those who are committed to making you wrong.

20. If you can at least please yourself in the situation, do so.

21. Do not attempt to deal with a problem in a way that will only create another one.

22. If jumping in too quickly, talking too soon, or blurting out inappropriate information tends to get you into trouble, learn to wait, sit still, do nothing, be silent, and think it through—all the way to the end.

23. Do not make yourself vulnerable to places or people who may not be safe for you, even if you think they should be.

24. If someone loves you just the way you are, and you happen to love him or her too, don't be too quick to turn it away.

25. Spend less energy on what you aren't getting and more on what you are getting.

26. If you're tired of doing everything alone, sit down and let someone else be there for you.

27. Have someone you can call to laugh and cry about it all when you need to.

28. Above all, keep your sense of humor. You haven't really lost if you still have that.

YOUR PROBLEM IS A GIFT

There is a "gift" in every situation and every interaction we ever have. Some of these gifts come as people and situations that make it easier to love ourselves, and some of these gifts seem to make it harder. The purpose of these gifts is to help us see if we should move closer to another person with all our heart and energy, or move away and be loving from a more detached position, so we can love others and ourselves better in the process.

Whatever dilemma you are in right now is a gift. View it from as many perspectives as you can. Then choose the route that will most benefit you—and others, if possible—in the long run. As much as you can, let the no-win traps stay behind. They always will be there waiting for those who want to sign up. Start from wherever you are now and make the very best of each moment, for that's all you have.

Only you can choose what to do in this moment. If you want, you can make it one of the best you ever had. Choose a thought that will bring you peace and freedom. Perhaps you'll choose to forgive. Perhaps you'll let go. Perhaps you will choose to see a situation from another person's point of view. Whatever you do, choose to believe your needs will be met; that the process, in fact, is happening already.

Make a decision that moves you into a life that is truly good for you, a life that reflects who you really are.

Bibliography

The American Heritage Dictionary of the English Language, 4th ed. Wilmington, Massachusetts: Houghton Mifflin, 2000.

Bateson, Gregory. *Steps to an Ecology of Mind*. Chicago and London: University of Chicago Press, 2000.

Berne, Eric. *Games People Play*. New York: Grover Press, 1964.

Erikson, Erik. *Childhood & Society*. Scranton, Pennsylvania: W.W. Norton & Co, Inc., 1993.

Ferrini, Paul. *The Silence of the Heart*. Greenfield, Massachusetts: Heartways Press, 1996.

Hay, Louise L. *You Can Heal Your Life*. Carson, California: Hay House, Inc., 1984.

McGraw, Philip, C. *Life Strategies*. New York: Hyperion, 1999.

Nelson, Portia, *There's a Hole in My Sidewalk*. Hillsboro, Oregon: Beyond Words Publishing, Inc., 1993.

Shelton, Cary L. *Double Binds: Finding the Spot Between the Rock and the Hard Place*. Anchorage, Alaska: Publication Consultants, 2000.

Wegscheider-Cruse, Sharon. *Learning to Love Yourself: Finding Your Self-Worth*. Deerfield Beach, Florida: Health Communications, Inc., 1987.

Suggested Reading

Bloomfield, Harold H., with Leonard Felder. *Making Peace with Your Parents: The Key to Enriching Your Life and All Your Relationships.* New York: Ballantine Books, 1985.

Braiker, Harriet B. *The Disease to Please.* New York: McGraw-Hill, 2001.

Canfield, Jack, Mark Victor Hansen, Patty Aubery, and Chrissy and Mark Donnelly. *Chicken Soup for the Working Woman's Soul.* Deerfield Beach, Florida: HCI, 2003.

Cameron, Julia, and Mark Bryan. *Money Drunk, Money Sober: 90 Days to Financial Freedom.* New York: Ballantine Wellspring, 1993.

Chopra, Deepak. *The Path to Love.* New York: Harmony Books, 1997.

DeAngelis, Barbara. *Are You the One for Me?* New York: Delacorte Press, 1992.

Elkaim, Mony. *If You Love Me, Don't Love Me.* New Jersey: Jason Aronson, Inc., 1997.

Ferrini, Paul. *Return to the Garden: Reflections of the Christ Mind,* Part 4. Greenfield, Massachusetts: Heartways Press, 1998.

Freeman, Arthur, and Rose DeWolf. *Woulda, Coulda, Shoulda: Overcoming Regrets, Mistakes, and Missed Opportunities.* New York: Harper Perennial, 1990.

Friedman, Martha. *Overcoming the Fear of Success.* New York: Warner Books, 1982.

Goldstine, Daniel, Katherine Larner, Shirley Zuckerman, and Hillary Goldstine. *The Dance Away Lover.* New York: Ballantine Books, 1978.

Goleman, Daniel. *Emotional Intelligence.* Audiotape. Audio Renaissance Tapes, Los Angeles, California, 1995.

Haley, Jay. *Leaving Home: The Therapy of Disturbed Young People.* New York: McGraw-Hill, 1980.

Hallowell, Edward M., and John J. Ratey. *Driven to Distraction.* New York: Simon & Schuster, 1995.

Hendricks, Gaylord, and Kathlyn Hendricks. *At the Speed of Life: A New Approach to Personal Change through Body-Centered Therapy.* New York: Bantam Books, 1993.

Jampolsky, Gerald G. *Love Is Letting Go of Fear.* New York: Bantam Books, 1981.

Johnson, Spencer. *"Yes" or "No": The Guide to Better Decisions.* New York: Harper Collins, 1992.

Kreisman, Jerold J., and Hal Straus. *I Hate You, Don't Leave Me.* New York: Avon Books, 1991.

Laing, Sam and Geri. *Friends & Lovers.* Missouri: Discipleship Publications International, 1996.

Levine, Michael. *The Address Book.* New York: Perigee Books, 1995.

Love, Patricia. *What to Do When a Parent's Love Rules Your Life.* New York: Bantam Books, 1991.

Lunden, Joan. *Wake-Up Calls.* New York: McGraw-Hill, 2001.

Matthews, Arlene Modica. *If I Think about Money So Much, Why Can't I Figure It Out?* New York: Summit Books, 1991.

Mellody, Pia, with Andrea Wells Miller and J. Keith Miller. *Facing Codependence.* San Francisco: Harper & Row, 1989.

Mountrose, Phillip, and Jane Mountrose. *Getting Thru to Your Emotions with EFT.* Arroyo Grande, California: Holistic Communications, 2000.

Mountrose, Phillip, and Jane Mountrose. *Getting Thru to Your Soul: The Four Keys to Living Your Divine Purpose.* Arroyo Grande, California: Holistic Communications, 2000.

Okimoto, Jean Davies, and Phyllis Jackson Stegall. *Boomerang Kids: How to Live with Adult Children Who Return Home.* Boston: Little, Brown and Company, 1987.

Paul, Jordan and Margaret. *Do I Have to Give Up Me to Be Loved by You?* Minneapolis: CompCare Publishers, 1983.

Paul, Margaret. *Inner Bonding: Becoming a Loving Adult to Your Inner Child.* San Francisco: Harper Collins, 1990.

Peck, Scott. *People of the Lie.* New York: Simon & Schuster Adult Publishing Group, 1997

Roberts, Monty. *Horse Sense For People.* New York, Viking, 2001.

Ruggiero, Vincent Ryan. *Feelings: A Guide to Critical Thinking.* Mountain View, California: Mayfield Publishing Company, 1984.

Russell, A. J. *God Calling, God at Eventide.* Uhrichsville, Ohio: Barbour and Company, 1994.

Schnall, Maxine. *What Doesn't Kill You Makes You Stronger.* Cambridge, Massachusetts: Perseus Books Group, 2002.

Schwab, Charles R. *You're Fifty—Now What?* New York: Three River Press, 2001.

Solden, Sari. *Women with Attention Deficit Disorder.* Grass Valley, California: Underwood Books, 1995.

Steiner, Claude. *Games Alcoholics Play.* New York: Ballantine Books, 1974.

Stoop, David. *Self Talk: Key to Personal Growth.* Old Tappan, New Jersey: Fleming H. Revell Company, 1973.

Tipping, Colin C. *Radical Forgiveness.* Marietta, Georgia: Global 13 Publications Co., Trust, 1997.

Tolle, Eckhart. *Stillness Speaks.* Novato, California & Vancouver, Canada: New World Library & Namaste Publishing, 2003.

Trafford, Abigail. *Crazy Time: Surviving Divorce and Building a New Life.* New York: Harper Perennial, 1992.

Udupa, K. N. *Stress and Its Management by Yoga.* Delhi, India: Motilal Banarsidass Publishers Limited, 2000.

Vanzant, Iyanla. *One Day My Soul Just Opened Up.* New York: Simon & Schuster, 1998.

Wetzler, Scott. *Living with the Passive Aggressive Man.* New York: Simon & Schuster, 1992.

Index

About the Author

Barbara Cowan Berg has a master's degree in clinical social work and practices psychotherapy in the state of California. She is also a consultant and lecturer and frequently appears on radio and television. She lives in Alta Loma, near Los Angeles, California.